PATHFINDER MODULE

Authors · James Jacobs, F. Wesley Schneider, Neil Spicer, and Greg A. Vaughan
Development Lead · Ron Lundeen
Cover Artist · Kiki Moch Rizky
Interior Artists · Sally Gottschalk, Gabriela Marchioro, Artur Nakhodkin, and Chenthooran Nambiarooran
Cartographer · Rob Lazzaretti

Creative Directors · James Jacobs, Robert G. McCreary, and Sarah E. Robinson
Director of Game Design · Jason Bulmahn
Managing Developers · Adam Daigle and Amanda Hamon Kunz
Organized Play Lead Developer · John Compton
Developers · Eleanor Ferron, Jason Keeley, Luis Loza, Ron Lundeen, Joe Pasini, Michael Sayre, Chris S. Sims, and Linda Zayas-Palmer
Starfinder Design Lead · Owen K.C. Stephens
Starfinder Society Developer · Thurston Hillman
Senior Designer · Stephen Radney-MacFarland
Designers · Logan Bonner and Mark Seifter
Managing Editor · Judy Bauer
Senior Editor · Christopher Carey
Editors · James Case, Leo Glass, Lyz Liddell, Adrian Ng, Lacy Pellazar, and Jason Tondro
Art Director · Sonja Morris
Senior Graphic Designers · Emily Crowell and Adam Vick
Production Artist · Tony Barnett
Franchise Manager · Mark Moreland
Project Manager · Gabriel Waluconis

Publisher · Erik Mona
Paizo CEO · Lisa Stevens
Chief Operations Officer · Jeffrey Alvarez
Chief Financial Officer · John Parrish
Chief Technical Officer · Vic Wertz
Director of Sales · Pierce Watters
Sales Associate · Cosmo Eisele
Vice President of Marketing & Licensing · Jim Butler
Marketing Manager · Dan Tharp
Licensing Manager · Glenn Elliott
Public Relations Manager · Aaron Shanks
Organized Play Manager · Tonya Woldridge
Human Resources Generalist · Megan Gilchrist
Accountant · Christopher Caldwell
Data Entry Clerk · B. Scott Keim
Web Production Manager · Chris Lambertz
Senior Software Developer · Gary Teter
Webstore Coordinator · Rick Kunz

Customer Service Team · Sharaya Copas, Katina Davis, Virginia Jordan, Sara Marie, Samantha Phelan, and Diego Valdez
Warehouse Team · Laura Wilkes Carey, Will Chase, Mika Hawkins, Heather Payne, Jeff Strand, and Kevin Underwood
Website Team · Brian Bauman, Robert Brandenburg, Whitney Chatterjee, Erik Keith, and Andrew White

ON THE COVER

Kyra faces the festering spirit of Haramil, an ancient horselord chieftain, in this exciting cover illustration by Kiki Moch Rizky.

Cradle of Night

TABLE OF CONTENTS

REFERENCE

This book refers to several other Pathfinder Roleplaying Game products using the following abbreviations, though these additional supplements are not required to make use of this book. Readers interested in references to Pathfinder RPG hardcovers can find the complete rules of these books available online for free at **paizo.com/prd**.

Advanced Player's Guide	APG	*Horror Adventures*	HA
Bestiary 2	B2	*Ultimate Combat*	UC
Bestiary 4	B4	*Ultimate Equipment*	UE
Bestiary 5	B5	*Ultimate Magic*	UM

paizo®

Paizo Inc.
7120 185th Ave NE, Ste 120
Redmond, WA 98052-0577

paizo.com

Cradle of Night

Advancement Track

Cradle of Night is designed for four characters using the Medium XP track.

8 The PCs begin the adventure at 8th level.

9 The PCs should be 9th level after retaking Aiyana's estate.

10 The PCs should reach 10th level before attempting to infiltrate the Forsaken Fane.

Adventure Summary

A caligni bard named Aiyana suspects that a magical item of great historical import to her people—the legendary *Cradle of Night*—lies hidden in an old cairn in northern Nidal. She worries that a faction of sinister cultists from her subterranean home city of Lyrudrada intends to steal the artifact for its own nefarious plans. When the PCs enter the cairn, they learn that not only have the cultists already stolen the *Cradle of Night*, but lingering energies from the artifact have infused the PCs with a corruption from the Shadow Plane. To unravel the cult's plans for the *Cradle of Night* and save themselves from the shadow curse, the PCs must venture to the dark folk city of Lyrudrada, aid Aiyana against the growing power of the cult, and infiltrate the cult's imposing temple-fortress. Once inside, the PCs must finally confront the architect of their worsening condition and undo a powerful outsider's plans for being reborn as a murderous demigod from the Shadow Plane.

INTRODUCTION

CHAPTER 1:
REMNANTS OF THE DARK

CHAPTER 2:
GAME OF SHADOWS

CHAPTER 3:
FATE OF THE FORSAKEN

APPENDIX 1:
LYRUDRADA

APPENDIX 2:
BESTIARY

Adventure Background

Ten thousand years ago, Earthfall shook every culture on the planet, and the resulting Age of Darkness set civilization itself teetering on the brink of annihilation. Seers from the doomed trading outpost of Calignos in the Mindspin Mountains determined a mere day before Earthfall that their city would be destroyed. They led an evacuation of their people, known as the caligni (a diverse group composed of elves, gnomes, half-elves, halflings, humans, and others), into the Darklands. Hoping to rely upon the subterranean realm of Nar-Voth as a temporary shelter, the caligni found themselves imprisoned when Earthfall collapsed the tunnels to the surface. They were forced ever downward in search of safety and resources.

As the caligni delved deeper belowground, the growing conviction that the gods had utterly abandoned them drove their seers to seek new gods for support and inspiration. A mysterious pantheon of Shadow Plane demigods known as the Forsaken responded to these prayers with unexpected—but far from unwelcome—vigor. The Forsaken bestowed potent magical gifts upon the caligni seers: smooth spheres of blackness known as the *Cradles of Night*. These artifacts infused the seers with shadowy power and spread that power outward to all caligni who offered their devotion to the Forsaken, reshaping them into new creatures adapted to their lightless home. What the caligni didn't realize was that the favor granted by the *Cradles of Night* concealed another purpose: the Forsaken drew upon their worshippers in a bid to escape the Shadow Plane. Before the Forsaken could act upon this plan, however, the demigods faced their own mysterious cataclysm, and most of the *Cradles of Night* shattered. The caligni once again found themselves without gods.

In only a few years, new patrons appeared before the caligni: owbs—half-humanoid presences who stepped from the shadows to offer aid in return for devotion. As time progressed, the owbs' influence bolstered the caligni, transforming the members of each new generation into the subcategories of caligni that exist today.

By this time, the caligni had largely forgotten their own history, thanks to generations of blind obedience first to the Forsaken and later to the owbs. The surface world became an object of myth and legend to them. The few remaining *Cradles of Night* were secretly kept by covetous masters, and tales of the Forsaken were eventually forgotten. In the world above, Golarion's recovery from the Age of Darkness that followed Earthfall went unnoticed and unseen by the caligni, and the people of Calignos slipped from the memory of the neighboring tribes of nomadic horselords. These nomads had long battled monstrous humanoids and fell creatures to maintain control of their homeland, so when the caligni eventually turned their attentions upward, they found themselves opposed by a well-entrenched enemy suspicious of all outsiders. Time and time again the caligni, known on the surface as dark

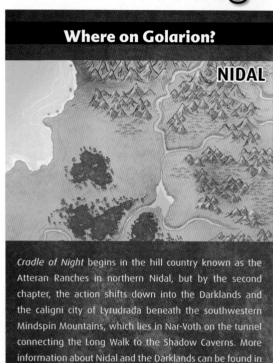

Where on Golarion?

NIDAL

Cradle of Night begins in the hill country known as the Atteran Ranches in northern Nidal, but by the second chapter, the action shifts down into the Darklands and the caligni city of Lyrudrada beneath the southwestern Mindspin Mountains, which lies in Nar-Voth on the tunnel connecting the Long Walk to the Shadow Caverns. More information about Nidal and the Darklands can be found in *Pathfinder Campaign Setting: The Inner Sea World Guide* and *Pathfinder Campaign Setting: Into the Darklands*.

folk, clashed with the horselords during nighttime raids but retreated back down into the dark.

Eventually, a vengeful horselord chieftain named Haramil led a pursuit of the fleeing caligni, intent on ending the threat for future generations of his people. Haramil and his warriors devastated the caligni and assaulted their temple, an edifice known as the Forsaken Fane. There, Haramil struck down several powerful owbs and caligni priests and looted the temple treasury of potent magical treasures, including an ancient orb of solid black stone—one of the few surviving *Cradles of Night*. This artifact magically extended Haramil's life, augmented his strength, and bound his wounds with shadowy power. When he finally fell in battle, Haramil was interred in a cairn near Barrowmoor along with many trophies from his opponents—including his sinister *Cradle of Night* (which his followers regarded with a mixture of fear and awe, and were relieved to bury for good).

Centuries after Haramil's attack, the dark folk returned to the site of the Forsaken Fane. They built a new society in the caverns surrounding the ruined temple, leaving the edifice itself as a taboo monument that they feared to enter. By the advent of the Age of Lost Omens, this region had grown into a city by the name of Lyrudrada, one of the largest dark folk settlements in the Darklands. And there the dark folk would have been content to dwell, were it not for the rise of a cult known as the Reborn, a haunted oracle named Nephenie, and a power-hungry owb prophet named Veilisendri.

Chapter 1

Remnants of the Dark

Caligni have always viewed death very differently than other races do, for when caligni expire, their bodies vanish in a violent display. The concept of a tomb is alien to caligni, for there are no physical remnants to inter when one of their kind dies. Undeath holds no real dread for the caligni. Cannibalism is all but unheard of. And with no body remaining after death, there is nothing physical from a departed loved one to cling to but memories and belongings. Caligni are no strangers to the concept of a dead body, for they are a violent people and their victims are numerous, but to some caligni the fact that they themselves leave nothing behind when they die is proof of their superiority over other races.

The Reborn take these beliefs to a new extreme. A secretive society originally based in the southern caverns of Lyrudrada, the Reborn assert that when caligni die, fragments of their memories pass on to their children while their souls move on to the afterlife. The violent flash of energy upon death is, they argue, a physical manifestation of this split between memory and soul. According to the Reborn, most caligni cannot recall these ancestral memories except in dreams or on an instinctual level. The Reborn claim otherwise for themselves. They claim they can recall ancestral memories dating all the way back to Earthfall, when their own direct ancestors, the Seers of Calignos, first led their people into the Darklands. In truth, the Reborn doctrine is a sham intended to give a group of arrogant caligni a reason to see themselves as superior to others of their kind; however, they cling to their doctrine with such tenacity that many of their members have come to believe their own thoughts are in fact ancestral memories. Until recently, the Reborn were merely a harmless (if self-important and egotistical) secret society. But when the mysterious oracle Nephenie joined the Reborn—and actually had the abilities claimed in their doctrine—the secret society expanded into a full-blown cult determined to dominate caligni society.

Nephenie truly did harbor the memories of her ancestors—in fact, she was haunted by them. While voices from many of her ancestors echoed in her mind, one voice in particular carried more weight than the others: that of Zenophys, a priest of an owb prophet named Veilisendri, slain by Haramil when the warlord stormed the Forsaken Fane so many centuries ago. The owbs who mold the caligni themselves serve greater masters, and owb prophets grant divine power carefully hoarded from the lost demigods called the Forsaken. Through Zenophys's memories, Veilisendri called to Nephenie and prompted her to break one of Lyrudrada's only taboos—entering the cursed ruins of the Forsaken Fane. Nephenie was tested sorely therein, but the combination of her oracular powers and whispers from her ancestors gave her the edge she needed to reach the fane's inner sanctum. Once there, she met the owb prophet Veilisendri, who had been trapped within the fane since its fall.

Nephenie emerged from the Forsaken Fane with a shadowy corruption upon her soul and a newfound purpose: she would help Veilisendri increase further in power and be reborn as one of the Forsaken demigods. The owb prophet needed two things to achieve this goal. First, he needed a robust cult, so that petitioners forged from the souls of its faithful would begin to gather on the Shadow Plane. Second, he needed one of the original artifacts the Forsaken had granted to the caligni: a *Cradle of Night*. The first goal was the easiest; Nephenie knew of the Reborn, and it was a relatively simple task for the charismatic caligni to convince the Reborn that she embodied their philosophy and could open the doorway to further power. In only a few years, Nephenie had transformed the Reborn into a full-fledged cult devoted to Veilisendri and had expanded its membership. She assumed leadership of the Reborn, and under her command, the cult emerged from the shadows to lay claim to the Forsaken Fane as its domain.

This act threw the already tumultuous city of Lyrudrada into true anarchy, providing a perfect background for the Reborn to recruit desperate and impressionable caligni to their cause. Those who converted to worship of Veilisendri were granted the right to dwell on the city's central island—close to the sacred Forsaken Fane itself—as well as protection, food, and luxuries. With his powers expanding, Veilisendri called forth powerful shadow creatures from deeper in the Darklands and even from the Outer Planes to bolster the cult's strength.

What's in a Name?

The word "caligni" (the plural and singular are the same) harkens back to the Azlanti outpost city of Calignos, the source of the race of humanoids known collectively to most surface dwellers as dark folk. These humanoids don't refer to themselves in that way, instead preferring to identify as all belonging to the caligni race, despite the fact that very few of their number know the source of the word, or the ancient history of their people. To them, there is little confusion between referring to all of their kind as caligni while also referring to the 0-HD caligni first presented on page 66 of *Pathfinder RPG Bestiary 5*, and indeed many caligni are offended at being called "dark folk." For the sake of rules clarity, the phrase "dark folk" is used in this adventure for the specific humanoid subtype as needed, but the word "caligni" is used elsewhere.

Once the cult was firmly established, Nephenie's task turned to the recovery of a *Cradle of Night*, a task made nearly impossible by the fact that most of the *Cradles of Night* had shattered when the Forsaken disappeared long ago. But calling upon the ancestral memories that still haunted her, Nephenie learned that a surviving *Cradle of Night* lay within the tomb of the man who slew her ancestor.

As Nephenie began her plans for the recovery of the *Cradle of Night* from Haramil's tomb, the power of the Reborn continued to grow in Lyrudrada. The city's caste-clans—delicately balanced in power before the rise of the Reborn—now fought viciously against one another while vying for the cult's favor. Only the caligni in the city's Bleakshore district saw the Reborn for what they truly were: a self-serving cult whose rule over Lyrudrada would result only in the city's destruction from within. A secret council of rebels formed in Bleakshore, and when their spies learned of Nephenie's plan to travel to the surface world and recover a legendary caligni artifact from a human tomb, they knew they had to act swiftly. The Bleakshore Council members knew that if they were to have any hope of opposing the cult in the future, they needed to stop the Reborn from gaining the *Cradle of Night*, but the thought of traveling to the horrific sun-blasted surface world (the Overburn, as it is known to them) frightened most of them even more than the rising power of the Reborn. Only one of the rebels stepped up to the challenge: a bard named Aiyana, who had spent much of her youth wandering the surface world before returning to the Darklands to rejoin her family. Aiyana promised to travel to the surface, seek aid from heroes there, and prevent the cult from retrieving the artifact from Haramil's tomb. Meanwhile, the other rebels remaining behind in Lyrudrada began to organize the resistance against the increasingly powerful Reborn.

Getting Started

Cradle of Night begins when the caligni bard Aiyana contacts the PCs, whom she recruits to travel to Haramil's tomb in northern Nidal and oppose the Reborn by preventing the cultists from retrieving a powerful artifact. Aiyana knows northern Nidal well, as she spent several years working with the church of Desna to smuggle people in and out of Nidal, and she has many old friends to help her locate likely heroes. As 8th-level characters, the PCs have doubtless already accomplished much to spread their fame, and Aiyana hears about the PCs, whether or not they are presently active in Nidal. She had previously obtained several *scrolls of shadow walk* to aid in her surface travels, and she still has two remaining when she finally tracks the PCs down to meet with them.

The staging of Aiyana's meeting should be tailored to fit your campaign. If the PCs have their own headquarters or base of operations in the area, Aiyana approaches them there. If the PCs are based farther away or are relatively nomadic, she may contact one of their NPC allies to set up a meeting. She is eager to earn the PCs' aid and trust, and as such you should strive to present her as respectful, honest, and friendly in her approach. If it appears the PCs will be more receptive to meeting with her if there's an obvious reward involved, make sure she lets the PCs know from the outset that she's willing to pay in advance for their aid. She prefers to meet after dark or indoors due to her sensitive eyes, but she agrees to meet elsewhere if dark environs make the PCs nervous or suspicious.

Aiyana is a slender woman with ash-gray skin who dresses in studded leather and colorful silks during her travels in the surface world. These colorful silks help to hide her unusual skin coloration in regions where intolerance holds sway while simultaneously bolstering her own morale—the city of Lyrudrada is a pretty bleak place to live, after all. She speaks with no accent save for when she's stressed or excited, at which time her words take on a hard, clipped cadence. Her faith in Desna has bolstered her natural curiosity about exotic locations, and she enjoys comparing and trading stories of her travels in the Darklands with others who've traveled extensively across the surface world. Aiyana's statistics are presented below.

Aiyana

AIYANA	CR 5

XP 1,600

Female caligni bard 6 (*Pathfinder RPG Bestiary 5* 66)

CG Medium humanoid (dark folk)

Init +2; **Senses** see in darkness; Perception +9

DEFENSE

AC 18, touch 13, flat-footed 15 (+4 armor, +2 Dex, +1 dodge, +1 shield)

hp 36 (6d8+6)

Fort +2, **Ref** +7, **Will** +5; +4 vs. bardic performance, language-dependent, and sonic

Weaknesses light sensitivity

OFFENSE

Speed 30 ft.

Melee mwk longsword +6 (1d8+1/19–20)

Ranged *+1 shortbow* +7 (1d6+1/×3)

Special Attacks bardic performance 7 rounds/day (countersong, distraction, fascinate [DC 16], inspire competence +2, inspire courage +2, *suggestion* [DC 16]), death throes

Bard Spells Known (CL 6th; concentration +9)

2nd (4/day)—*blindness/deafness* (DC 15), *eagle's splendor*, *mirror image*, *suggestion* (DC 15)

1st (5/day)—*cure light wounds*, *feather fall*, *grease* (DC 14), *undetectable alignment* (DC 14)

INTRODUCTION

CHAPTER 1:
REMNANTS OF THE DARK

CHAPTER 2:
GAME OF SHADOWS

CHAPTER 3:
FATE OF THE FORSAKEN

APPENDIX 1:
LYRUDRADA

APPENDIX 2:
BESTIARY

0 (at will)—*detect magic*, *flare* (DC 13), *know direction*,
    mage hand, *message*, *read magic*

TACTICS

Before Combat Aiyana casts *undetectable alignment* on
    herself every day, but in the presence of those she hopes
    to ally with, she is forthcoming in letting them know she's
    used the spell, explaining that she relies on it to protect
    herself from enemies, not to deceive her potential friends.

During Combat Aiyana's first act in battle is to cast *mirror*
    image, followed by activating her bardic performance to
    inspire courage. If she's on her own, she remains mobile
    and uses her shortbow to fight, using Arcane Strike each
    round to bolster her damage. When fighting with allies, she
    adopts a support role, casting *cure light wounds* on injured
    allies or using spells such as *blindness/deafness*, *grease*,
    and *suggestion* to keep enemies from maintaining an
    organized offense.

Morale Aiyana won't abandon an ally in battle, and she fights
    to the death to protect those she cares about. When alone,
    she prefers to avoid combat entirely, relying upon her
    spells and acrobatic abilities to escape combat.

STATISTICS

Str 13, **Dex** 14, **Con** 10, **Int** 12, **Wis** 10, **Cha** 16

Base Atk +4; **CMB** +5; **CMD** 18

Feats Arcane Strike, Craft Wondrous Item, Dodge

Skills Acrobatics +11, Knowledge (dungeoneering) +9,
    Knowledge (history) +9, Knowledge (religion) +9,
    Perception +9, Perform (act) +12, Perform (wind
    instruments) +12, Sense Motive +9, Stealth +11

Languages Common, Dark Folk, Shadowtongue

SQ bardic knowledge +3, lore master 1/day, versatile
    performances (act, wind)

Combat Gear *scrolls of shadow walk* (2); **Other Gear** *+1*
    studded leather, mwk buckler, *+1 shortbow* with 20
    arrows, *sleep arrows* (4), mwk longsword, flute, master
    key to doors in Aiyana's estate, 47 gp

Aiyana's Request

Once she secures an audience with the PCs, Aiyana gets
right to the point. Read or paraphrase the following.

"Thank you for agreeing to this meeting; I've heard tell of your
exploits, and my people have need of your abilities. My name
is Aiyana, and I hail from the city of Lyrudrada, underneath the
southern reaches of your Mindspin Mountains. The people of
my city have long been capricious and unpredictable, but of
late they have fallen under the influence of a malign cult called
the Reborn—a cult I fear has dangerous plans.

"The Reborn seek a powerful artifact to aid them in
these plans: the Cradle of Night. We know very little about
this magical treasure, other than that it played a role in the
formation of my kind millennia ago and was said to allow the
manipulation of energies from the Shadow Plane. My peoples'
history is riddled with conflicts, and it shames me a bit to
admit that we, as a culture, have never excelled at preserving

ancestral lore. Specific details about the Cradle of Night have
been lost, but if the Reborn gain control of it, they'll learn of its
powers and master them soon enough—and to our detriment,
I fear.

"The Cradle of Night was stolen many centuries ago by a
human warlord named Haramil. My people and Haramil's
armies warred frequently in the distant past. Haramil ended
those wars decisively with a brutal assault on our city, and
among the treasures he took from the caligni was this Cradle
of Night. Records of how he used the artifact to bolster his
warmongering in the decades that followed are easier to find,
seeing as how you uplanders are so much better at maintaining
your histories.

"In any event, the Cradle of Night was buried with Haramil.
His allies were more than eager to be rid of it and move on
from his brutal reign, it would appear. And so there, in his tomb,
the artifact has rested for a long, long time. The Reborn know
what I know about the artifact; if they haven't sent agents to
retrieve it already, they will soon. I need strong-hearted and
willing adventurers to assist me in exploring Haramil's tomb.
I doubt we'll be able to destroy the Cradle of Night, but if we
can bolster its defenses, or at least prevent the Reborn from
claiming it, we can buy my allies the time they desperately
need to defeat the cult back in Lyrudrada.

"I hope you'll help me. I know you've no investment in a city
from the Darklands, but I've brought treasure to reward you in
advance for your assistance. And if you can help me save my
city from the Reborn, my allies will no doubt be more than
willing to reward you further!"

Aiyana is eager to answer questions—see Preliminary
Investigations for what the PCs can learn from her
and what they might learn themselves by attempting
Knowledge checks. Aiyana wants to set out for
Haramil's tomb as quickly as possible and informs the
PCs that she can use a *scroll of shadow walk* to expedite
the journey. She has also procured a map of the region
that shows the location of the tomb, a few nearby
villages, and the entrance she used to emerge from the
Darklands and onto the surface world. If the PCs prefer
some other method of travel to the tomb, Aiyana urges
speed, since the Reborn could be looting the tomb at
any moment. As it turns out, no matter how swiftly they
travel, the PCs and Aiyana are destined to arrive at the
tomb soon after the Reborn have claimed the *Cradle of*
Night for themselves.

Treasure: The treasure and magic items Aiyana
mentions to the PCs are no lie. Her fellow caligni may
have been unwilling to accompany her to the surface,
but they were certainly generous in giving up money and
gear to help Aiyana hire adventurers for aid. She hands
the payment over to the PCs as soon as they agree to
accompany her back to the tomb. This treasure consists
of 2,400 gp in various gemstones, a masterwork mithral
dagger, three *potions of cure moderate wounds*, three *potions*

Aiyana's Role

Cradle of Night assumes that Aiyana accompanies the PCs for the majority of the adventure and bolsters the party's support capabilities and recovery options. Aiyana's familiarity with caligni society, the history of her people, and some of the adventure sites will also give the PCs an edge. You shouldn't lower the XP the PCs earn while they adventure with Aiyana's aid, nor should you track XP for her. If you wish, you can level her up each time the average PC level increases. You should retain control of Aiyana's actions during the adventure, but play her with an eye toward being eager to follow the PCs' orders and suggestions. She shouldn't be a puppet of the PCs, as she has her own goals and motivations that drive her actions, but she understands that the PCs represent her best hope of restoring her city and preventing the rise of a powerful evil force.

If you'd rather have Aiyana take a smaller role in the adventure (perhaps to allow game play to focus more on the players), simply have her remain at a base camp while the PCs explore adventure sites. Note that since the encounters in this adventure skew slightly more challenging as a result of the assumption that Aiyana is accompanying the PCs, you might want to consider adjusting the encounter lethality slightly if Aiyana isn't with them.

If Aiyana dies or leaves the party, the adventure can continue as written, but the PCs will need to rely upon their own skills and motivation to continue onward. Player curiosity is a powerful force, as is the need to avenge the death of a fallen ally—you can use both of these to encourage the PCs to continue with the adventure. Alternately, you can use the shadowbound corruption that afflicts the PCs as a motivator by having visions of the *Cradle of Night* lure them to Lyrudrada.

by asterisks unprompted can be an excellent way to convey her helpfulness to the players beyond her role in presenting the quest to the PCs, and encourage them to value her companionship.

CRADLE OF NIGHT LORE

Knowledge (arcana or planes)

Check Result	Information Gained
DC 20*	There were once many *Cradles of Night*. These powerful artifacts were used by the caligni, but over the centuries all of them have been destroyed or lost. A *Cradle of Night* resembles a fist-sized black orb cloaked in shadow.
DC 25*	The *Cradles of Night* granted those who carried them power from the Shadow Plane, including increased strength, health, and healing capabilities. Although the bearer of a *Cradle of Night* isn't immortal, the artifact imparts a supernaturally long life span.
DC 30	The power of a *Cradle of Night* spread among the bearer's allies, whether or not the bearer willed it, and the influence of these artifacts is believed to have created the various distinct caligni races over time (which the surface races know as dark creepers, dark stalkers, and similar names).
DC 35	The *Cradles of Night* were gifts to the caligni long ago by a group of mysterious demigods known as the Forsaken. Caligni don't worship the Forsaken any longer, and these demigods vanished long ago. Their plans for caligni and the *Cradles of Night* remain unknown.

HARAMIL LORE

Knowledge (history or local)

Check Result	Information Gained
DC 15*	Haramil was a legendary warlord among the nomadic, Gozreh-worshipping horselords who dwelt in the hill country of northern Nidal during the Age of Destiny many millennia ago. These Kellid humans were powerful warriors with a culture centered around honor and tradition.
DC 20*	Haramil led a devastating assault against caligni raiders' Darklands home. Not only did he slay several of their

of lesser restoration, a *scroll of shadow conjuration*, and an ounce of *stone salve*, all carried in a *handy haversack*, which is itself part of the payment to the PCs.

Preliminary Investigations

The PCs may wish to research more about the *Cradle of Night*, the city of Lyrudrada, Haramil, or the Forsaken (once they learn of them) before or during the adventure. Presented here are the results of Knowledge checks to recall information, whether these checks are attempted by the PCs or by experts they consult. On a given check, the PCs learn all information with a DC equal to or less than the check result. Aiyana knows the information marked with an asterisk, and she can give the PCs that information if they ask her about the subject. In fact, having Aiyana supply the information indicated

INTRODUCTION

CHAPTER 1:
REMNANTS OF THE DARK

CHAPTER 2:
GAME OF SHADOWS

CHAPTER 3:
FATE OF THE FORSAKEN

APPENDIX 1:
LYRUDRADA

APPENDIX 2:
BESTIARY

leaders, but he stole a powerful artifact called the *Cradle of Night*. Legend holds that this artifact influenced him in sinister ways and drove him to abandon Gozreh's teachings.

DC 25*	The *Cradle of Night* granted Haramil a supernaturally extended life span and gifted him with increased strength and healing capabilities, but it also drove him to fits of fury and sadism. When Haramil finally died, he was buried in a tomb in the low mountains northwest of the Barrowmoor.
DC 30	Haramil's people feared him and loathed the *Cradle of Night*; they were not sad to see his cruel reign end when he died. Haramil was interred outside of the traditional burial grounds of his people due to fears his restless spirit or the *Cradle of Night* would spawn a plague of undeath and also as a way to condemn his legacy.

LYRUDRADA LORE
Knowledge (local)

Check Result	Information Gained
DC 15*	Lyrudrada is a caligni city that lies in the Darklands beneath the southern Mindspin Mountains. Centuries ago, it went to war with the horselords of Nidal and was subsequently sacked, though it has since risen again to prominence. It is not on the major trade routes of the Darklands, but Darklands traders of many races transact business in Lyrudrada, particularly in the neighborhood known as Trader's Rift.
DC 20*	The caste-clans of Lyrudrada have held an uneasy equilibrium of power for centuries. With the rise of the cult called the Reborn, though, that balance has been thrown into anarchy. This new faction has taken control of the central portions of the city around the lake at the city's heart. The Reborn cultists have earned the allegiance of several powerful creatures both native to the city and from other areas of the Darklands; some rumors insist that the cult has gained the services of a dark dragon from the Shadow Plane.
DC 25*	Lyrudrada is where the ancient caligni worship of a group of demigods known

as the Forsaken first originated, and the city holds the only known temple to those mysterious deities—though the temple has been considered taboo by the city's inhabitants for centuries. The Reborn cult has recently taken this temple as its headquarters.

DC 30	Lyrudrada is the oldest known caligni city and may actually be where they first originated during the Age of Darkness. The temple on its central island, called the Forsaken Fane, is said to hold secrets of the city's ancient past.

FORSAKEN LORE
Knowledge
(religion or planes)

Check Result	Information Gained
DC 30	Before owbs sought dominion over caligni, shadowy deities known as the Forsaken held sway over dark folk. Universally evil, the Forsaken encouraged worship from carefully selected mortal races for their own inscrutable ends. Worship of the Forsaken died out ages ago and has long been forgotten among caligni.
DC 35	The Forsaken saved the fleeing refugees of the surface city of Calignos from the destruction of Earthfall. It was from these survivors who fled into the Darklands and embraced the darkness that the first dark folk—caligni—were created.
DC 40	The Forsaken molded caligni in their image through the use of their *Cradles of Night*. They sought to harness the power of their worshippers' souls through the explosive destruction of caligni's mortal bodies upon death, and by harvesting their immortal essence within these artifacts. That all dark folk combust at the instant of their deaths is a lasting legacy of this meddling by the Forsaken.
DC 45	The Forsaken were equal to demigods in status, though they sought to become more through their patronage of the caligni race and their harvest of caligni's immortal essences. The Forsaken all vanished under mysterious circumstances long ago, and what became of these malign demigods is entirely unknown.

A. HARAMIL'S TOMB

When Haramil finally perished, his followers rejoiced. He had grown sinister and cruel after decades spent under the influence of the *Cradle of Night*, and with his death, his followers were able to bury both him and the artifact and put the tyrant's reign behind them. Out of fear that Haramil's evil might taint the cairns of their other heroes and leaders, and as a way to subtly indicate that they didn't consider Haramil worthy of such legendary company, these followers didn't inter Haramil in the Barrowmoor, the ancestral burial ground of their leaders. However, they could not deny that such a fearsome leader as Haramil deserved a lavish tomb to commemorate his many victories. They hoped that a large, trap-laden tomb might ensure that Haramil's spirit and the *Cradle of Night* both remained safely consigned to the earth. They therefore built Haramil's tomb 15 miles to the west of the Barrowmoor and hid both his body and the artifact inside. Aiyana already knows the location of Haramil's tomb, but the PCs can confirm its location with a successful DC 25 Knowledge (history or local) check.

Aiyana hopes that she and the PCs can reach the tomb before agents of the Reborn arrive. She wants to determine whether the *Cradle of Night* is truly buried in Haramil's tomb and, if it is, either bolster the tomb's defenses or move the artifact to a more secure location. Aiyana believes that her contacts in the church of Desna would be a good option for a secure location, although she's willing to entertain suggestions from the PCs—who may recommend removing it from Nidal entirely. In the end, these discussions amount to very little—by the time the PCs arrive at Haramil's tomb, the Reborn have already come and gone. They were forced to destroy many of the wards in the tomb to plunder the *Cradle of Night*, and these acts have resulted in the entire complex becoming enshrouded with energies and sinister predators from the Shadow Plane. This intrusion has also torn Haramil's spirit into three distinct parts, each of which haunts a separate section of the tomb.

Regardless of how quickly the PCs work to reach the tomb, they arrive a day after the departure of the Reborn forces. The massive stone doors that once barred entrance to the tomb hang ajar and shrouded in deep shadow. This should be the first indication that the PCs have arrived too late—an indication confirmed by further investigation of the tomb's interior—but Aiyana clings to the hope that the Reborn might still be in the tomb and that the PCs might still be able to confront them before the *Cradle of Night* is lost. Only in the innermost vault is Aiyana forced to admit that they are, indeed, too late.

Features of Haramil's Tomb

As long as any of the three fragments of Haramil's spirit remain active in the tomb, the tomb retains a supernatural connection to the Shadow Plane. The tomb's interior remains in dim light at all times, the corners of each room infested with strangely shifting shadows cast by a faint light from no apparent source. Light sources brought into the tomb provide illumination no stronger than dim light. Any spellcaster attempting to cast a spell with the light or darkness descriptor while within Haramil's tomb must succeed at a DC 20 caster level check or lose the spell. Even if the check is successful, the spell's effects manifest at the PC's caster level – 1. *Continual flame* spells cast within the tomb have their durations reduced to 1 hour per caster level. A PC who succeeds at a DC 20 Knowledge (arcana or planes) check determines these effects and influences after 1 minute of study. Creatures from the Shadow Plane and humanoids with the dark folk subtype can cast these spells in Haramil's tomb without penalty, as can creatures with a shadowbound corruption (as described in Becoming Corrupted below).

The tomb's chambers and passageways are crafted from hewn stone (hardness 8, hp 540, break DC 50, Climb DC 20), as are all doors within (hardness 8, hp 60, break DC 28). The ceilings within the tomb are uniformly 9 feet high, except where indicated.

Becoming Corrupted

The shadowy energies that have infused Haramil's tomb as a result of the theft of the *Cradle of Night* present both a danger and an opportunity to the PCs. Once they step within the shadowy penumbra that extends out into area **A1**, the PCs unknowingly take on the corruption of the Shadow Plane. This corruption is subtle at first—while the PCs will surely notice the influence dimming any light sources they bring into Haramil's tomb, they won't immediately realize that these energies are dimming their own life forces as well.

This influence grants each PC the shadowbound corruption, as detailed on pages 34–35 of *Pathfinder RPG Horror Adventures*. There is no saving throw to avoid this corruption; it automatically influences all who enter Haramil's tomb in the days after the *Cradle of Night* was stolen away by the Reborn (save those who already have links to the Shadow Plane—caligni, such as Aiyana, are not affected by the corruption). A few days after the PCs become exposed, the lingering corruption in Haramil's tomb fades as the tear between the Shadow Plane and this world heals. While those who became shadowbound earlier remain corrupted, the tomb poses no further threat to additional visitors.

Every PC gains eerie perception (*Horror Adventures* 34) as an initial manifestation from this corruption, including both the gift and the stain, although the timing of when this manifestation becomes apparent to the players is flexible. This manifestation should become evident at a dramatic point after all members of the party have been exposed (in other words, at a point after which every member has entered Haramil's tomb) and a PC

Cradle of Night

INTRODUCTION

CHAPTER 1:
REMNANTS OF THE DARK

CHAPTER 2:
GAME OF SHADOWS

CHAPTER 3:
FATE OF THE FORSAKEN

APPENDIX 1:
LYRUDRADA

APPENDIX 2:
BESTIARY

is hampered by the supernatural illumination within the tomb. For example, when a PC misses a foe due to the miss chance granted by dim light, or when a spellcaster PC fails to cast a spell with the light or darkness descriptor, that PC's manifestation suddenly appears. This manifestation should occur the instant before the attack or spell would have failed, causing the PC to succeed instead. If an appropriate triggering event does not occur on its own, it should occur when the PCs first encounter one of the undead fragments of Haramil's spirit in areas **A7**, **A9**, or **A10**.

Once the first manifestation occurs, it catalyzes the corruption in the other PCs so that all of them gain the eerie perception gift and stain simultaneously. The PCs can confirm that the condition is caused by a shadowbound corruption with a successful DC 20 Knowledge (arcana or planes) check. A success also provides the basic information about corruptions generally, as provided in *Horror Adventures*.

This shadowbound corruption begins at stage 0, and the PCs have a month to seek a cure for the corruption before they need to worry about its natural progression to later stages. While corrupted PCs feel slightly unsettled in the presence of great beauty or goodness (potentially including their own), they do not feel the need to destroy beauty or goodness, and they take no in-game penalties from their unsettled feeling for the duration of this initial month. This should be enough time for the party to finish the adventure and, hopefully, remove their corruption by thwarting the owb prophet Veilisendri, recovering the *Cradle of Night*, and destroying the artifact.

It's likely that the PCs will be concerned and curious about their corruption. Aiyana knows enough about the condition to justify the players familiarizing themselves with the rules for corruptions, but she's not sure how the PCs can magnify or remove their condition. She mentions that she knows a scholar of shadow magic back in her home city of Lyrudrada—an information broker named Shevarimarr. Aiyana suggests that if the PCs accompany her home after exploring Haramil's tomb, they can consult with Shevarimarr for more information (see area **D**). A PC who succeeds at a DC 20 Knowledge (arcana or planes) check realizes that if the *Cradle of Night* was responsible for the shadowy energies that infuse Haramil's tomb, the key to removing the corruption may well lie with the artifact.

As the adventure progresses, the PCs face situations that may advance their shadowbound corruption and impart new manifestations (and their associated gifts and stains). This is particularly true when the PCs enter the Forsaken Fane and come into contact with its denizens, who are infused with the energies of the Shadow Plane (as detailed in Chapter 3). A PC exposed to further manifestation of a shadowbound corruption can attempt a Will save (DC = 15 + current manifestation level) to avoid gaining the manifestation level.

What If the PCs Don't Explore?

Once the PCs start to realize that they may well be too late to prevent the theft of the *Cradle of Night*, they might abandon further exploration of Haramil's tomb. Aiyana does her best to convince the PCs to keep exploring the tomb, clinging as long as she can to the hope that the Reborn might still be within and can be confronted. If she fails to convince the PCs to carry on—or if the PCs use divination magic or other means to conclusively determine that the *Cradle of Night* has already been taken from the tomb—the adventure can still continue. In this case, Aiyana suggests visiting the information broker Shevarimarr in an attempt to learn more about the *Cradle of Night* before she asks the PCs to accompany her to her estate in Lyrudrada. If the PCs give up on Haramil's tomb after they've already acquired their shadowbound corruption, a desire to learn more about their condition may also compel them to seek out Shevarimarr in Lyrudrada.

Finally, if you feel that the inclusion of corruptions would be an unwelcome or awkward addition to your game table, you can simply ignore this element of *Cradle of Night* entirely. In this case, the PCs' motivation to continue the adventure focuses exclusively on the defeat of the malicious Reborn cult rather than on their own personal redemption from corruption.

A1. Tomb Entrance (CR 7)

Hills looming to either side of an overgrown trail cast shadows across the approach to Haramil's tomb. Next to an opening in the natural stone of the canyon wall, a few trees have taken root in the rocky soil. Beside them, massive stone doors have been set into the hillside. Though they presumably sealed the entrance at one time, it now stands open. An unsettling penumbra of gloomy illumination exudes from within, cloaking the area immediately surrounding the entrance with shifting shadows.

The influence of the Shadow Plane extends in a 20-foot-radius hemisphere from the open doors. The boundaries of this gloom are crisp and unsettling, leaving no mistake that they are supernatural in origin. Aiyana is particularly put off by this sight, as she'd expected the doors to the tomb to be not only closed tightly, but hidden from view—that they hang open and exude obvious shadows is the first clue that the Reborn have beaten her and the PCs to the tomb. Aiyana nonetheless encourages the party onward in hopes of catching the Reborn still within.

Creatures: A group of four shadows, lured across planar boundaries worn thin by the theft of the *Cradle of Night*, have gathered in the area just outside of the

tomb entrance. The four undead are fascinated by the strange light (be it night or day) at the edge of the shadowy region, but they have little interest in venturing into the world beyond for now. The shadows lurk amid the trees and hillside crags, swiftly moving to attack any who approach. While the shadows don't venture into the tomb itself on their own, they pursue any PCs who flee into the interior, at which point they may well attack living creatures within the complex—canny PCs could use this propensity against living monsters within the tomb if they note how eagerly the shadows follow them.

SHADOWS (4)	CR 3

XP 800 each
hp 19 each (*Pathfinder RPG Bestiary* 245)

A2. The Broken Seal (CR 10)

The black stone walls of this cylindrical chamber rise overhead to a height of thirty feet. Passageways lead east and west, while a stone double door blocks progress to the north and an open double door leads south. A ten-foot-radius circle of runes adorns the floor in the center of the room, but the etchings have been badly damaged by cracks and gouges.

The inscribed runes on the chamber floor once served as a focus to contain the *Cradle of Night's* influence within the tomb and to prevent Haramil's spirit from rising as a vengeful undead monster. The PCs can identify this purpose with a successful DC 20 Knowledge (arcana or religion) check, and on a success they also know that the damage done to the runes has rendered them useless. *Detect magic* and similar spells reveal only a lingering aura of abjuration magic extending from the ring of runes down the passages to the north, east, and west, but those lingering pathways of protection have evaporated. The damage to the runes appears to be very recent, and a PC who succeeds at a DC 15 Knowledge (engineering) or Survival check confirms that the tampering was intentional, and that it took place within the last couple of days.

Creatures: A pair of tenebrous worms that crept through the recent tears in reality in the tomb have taken up residence in this chamber. The creatures are hungry, but they haven't grown hungry enough yet to venture out into the unknown areas outside of this room. They know that the deathwebs lair to the east (area **A3**)—in fact, they barely managed to escape those lurking predators to make it here—but they haven't yet realized that a potential meal is in hiding in the chamber to the west (area **A4**). As a result, the two worms eagerly lurch to attack when the PCs enter this room.

If they aren't aware of the PCs' presence, one of the worms is writhing around on the circle of runes while the other is near the double door to the north. If they

have been alerted to nearby PCs—such as by sounds of combat against the shadows outside the tomb (area **A1**)—they have taken up position on either side of the southern door to ambush the first creature to enter the room.

Unwilling to let a prospective meal escape, these worms pursue foes who flee, and they fight to the death.

TENEBROUS WORMS (2)	CR 8

XP 4,800 each
hp 105 each (*Pathfinder RPG Bestiary 2* 260)

A3. Torn Shadows (CR 8)

Rocky debris and loose soil form much of this chamber's floor, obviously fallen from cracks and crevices in the ceiling fifteen feet overhead. Niches and hollows extend to the east and south, but these are filled with massive cobwebs infused with writhing shadows. A worked stone wall to the north bears a life-sized mural of an ancient warrior standing with a shield and lance. The curled-up corpses of four human-sized spiders lie on the ground of the cavern, casting strange shadows across the floor.

To save time in the tomb's construction, its builders chose this site due to the presence of an existing set of natural caverns in the hill. Most of the caves were expanded and finished with worked stone, resulting in the other areas of the tomb as they exist today, but this area was left unfinished. During construction, the chamber served as storage for tools and resources, as well as a concealed entry to the hidden shrine (area **A5**). This secret entrance is both well hidden and locked; finding it requires a successful DC 25 Perception check, and unlocking its ancient bolt mechanism requires a successful DC 25 Disable Device check.

The room's rough, uneven walls were a liability recently, for when the *Cradle of Night* was wrenched from Haramil's crypt (area **A10**), the resulting infusion of shadowy energies built up among the craggy, jagged walls of this cave to such an extent that they wore the boundaries between the Material Plane and the Shadow Plane thin. Hours after the Reborn left the tomb with the *Cradle of Night* in their clutches, this thinned boundary finally ruptured, spilling several denizens from the Shadow Plane into the vicinity while simultaneously overwhelming the giant spiders that had been dwelling in this chamber, transforming them into undead monsters (see Creatures on page 13).

The full-scale rupture between planes has mostly healed, but a *detect magic* spell cast here reveals strong conjuration magic throughout the chamber. A PC who succeeds at a DC 25 Knowledge (planes) check can confirm that this site recently hosted a planar rift that has since repaired itself.

The alcoves to the east and south are choked with dried webs. Although they ripple with strange shadows, they are

INTRODUCTION

CHAPTER 1:
REMNANTS OF THE DARK

CHAPTER 2:
GAME OF SHADOWS

CHAPTER 3:
FATE OF THE FORSAKEN

APPENDIX 1:
LYRUDRADA

APPENDIX 2:
BESTIARY

easy to destroy with fire or simply by pushing them aside. The back of each alcove contains only loose soil. The way the shadows shift and move in this room is unsettling, but it has no specific effect.

Creatures: Six giant burrowing spiders once nested in the web-filled niches to the east and south, having dug their way into the chamber from the hillside above. Of the six spiders, four were slain outright by the blast of shadowy power that flooded this room, but the remaining two, their bellies full of eggs, did more than die: they rose as deathwebs.

The undead spiders no longer have the need to feed and are content to linger in this room, basking in the rippling shadow. Once the tomb's shadowy influence completely fades, the deathwebs are likely to wander off, but they are content to remain here for now and attack anyone that intrudes upon their lair. The deathwebs attempt to restrain foes with their webs before moving in to attack with their bites. Dimly bound to their living habits of remaining close to their nests, the deathwebs don't leave this chamber, even to pursue fleeing foes.

DEATHWEBS (2)	CR 6

XP 2,400 each

hp 71 each (*Pathfinder RPG Bestiary 3* 65)

A4. Hall of Shame (CR 8)

A short stairway descends to this low chamber, where eight stone tables stand between several shallow alcoves. Each table bears ancient, dusty relics such as scrolls, armor, carved figurines, and jewelry; all are in various stages of disrepair. Detailed carvings of a furious man engaged in battle adorn the alcoves between each table.

While at first glance, this room appears to be a standard celebration of a bygone leader's accomplishments in life, closer examination reveals the truth: this hall records the shame of Haramil's tribe at their inability to stand up to their increasingly sadistic leader while he lived.

The PCs can identify Haramil in numerous places in the alcove carvings. In each, he is a furious-looking muscular man clad in chain mail and armed with either a sword or lance. His enemies and allies alike seem to fear his presence, and in many scenes, it's hard to tell friend from foe as Haramil hews through them all with fearsome rage. In every scene, Haramil clutches a small black sphere in one hand that shrouds him in coils of shadow: the *Cradle of Night*.

With a successful DC 20 Knowledge (history) check, a PC confirms that the people of Haramil's time often offered personal belongings or memorabilia as final gifts to the departed. On closer inspection, the "gifts" left for Haramil are more like insults, as if those who buried Haramil wanted to mock his passing and diminish his legacy. Each gift is fundamentally flawed in some way: a helmet is flimsy and lopsided, a ring contains an obvious fake gem in its setting, and a figurine of Haramil has comical and unflattering exaggerations. PCs who succeed at a DC 20 Sense Motive check understand that these offerings are all intended to be sly insults. In addition, the passage of many centuries has worn on these offerings, and none of the items displayed here are worth anything.

This room's only exit is the staircase, which leads up to area **A2**.

Creature: A shadow collector named Xermathiel happened to be in the right place at the right time while traveling across northern Nidal. When the Reborn stole the *Cradle of Night*, it released a surge of shadow energy. Xermathiel was drawn to this energy like a beacon, and he immediately diverted his trip to investigate. After observing the tomb from safety for a few hours, he entered using a combination of stealth and *shadow step* to avoid the denizens within. He's spent the last few hours in this room, fascinated by the images depicting Haramil bearing some sort of powerful shadowy magic. Xermathiel initially suspected that one of the objects in this room might bear some connection to the magic sphere the figure holds, but he's recently realized that the items here are as worthless as they initially appeared, and the shadowy orb might be elsewhere in the tomb.

Xermathiel isn't evil, but he is tenacious at pursuing leads regarding unusual magic items and he is very defensive of this find. If he hears trouble upstairs (such as a fight between PCs and tenebrous worms), he slips into the shadows behind the northwest table to bide his time. If the PCs don't appear within a reasonable amount of time, Xermathiel slips out of the room to track them, observing them while hiding in the shadows for as long as he's able.

Once he is discovered, Xermathiel attempts to trick the PCs, claiming to be the caretaker of this sacred tomb. His lack of knowledge about the tomb is a real liability—as he doesn't even know the name of the person entombed here—but he hopes to be able to either scare the PCs off so he can study the ruins in peace, or bully a tithe from them in the form of their shadows. If the PCs allow Xermathiel to steal their shadows, the delighted fey grants them permission to loot the rest of the tomb. In fact, he merely retreats to watch and wait, hoping the PCs deal with the tomb's defenses so that he can demand further tithes in the form of magic items when they try to leave.

XERMATHIEL	CR 8

XP 4,800

Male shadow collector (*Pathfinder RPG Bestiary 5* 228)

hp 90

TACTICS

During Combat Xermathiel has 4 shadow points when he

first encounters the PCs. In combat, he attempts to remain hidden or secure a good hiding place with *shadow step*. Once safely in hiding, he uses *shadow conjuration* to summon earth elementals. With his enemies distracted, he uses Spring Attack to stab opponents or attempts to steal their shadows. Xermathiel never uses his last shadow point in combat, instead saving it to aid his escape if things go badly.

Morale Xermathiel flees combat if reduced to fewer than 20 hit points, and he prefers to retreat by using *shadow walk*, as few foes can then catch him. Once he departs, he abandons this region entirely and does not return.

Treasure: Xermathiel was on his way to Pangolais in Nidal to pawn a collection of treasures he'd pilfered from an art merchant in Korvosa when he was distracted by Haramil's tomb. He carries this collection of treasures in a *bag of holding* (type I), a stash that includes five coral necklaces worth 250 gp each, three brass rings worth 50 gp each, a relatively small but exquisite portrait of Archbanker Darb Tuttle of Korvosa worth 1,200 gp, and a *scroll of true seeing*.

A5. Shrine of the Guardians (CR 9)

This hidden shrine can only be reached by locked secret doors located in areas **A3**, **A6**, and **A9**.

Arching ribs of stone support the fifteen-foot-high ceiling of this oval chamber. Tattered tapestries hang from curved walls to the east and west, each depicting a scene of natural fury—a devastating tornado to the east, and a looming tsunami to the west. The focus of each of these natural disasters seems to be a single humanoid shape cloaked in shadows.

The tomb's builders constructed this room as a secret bypass to the dangerous trap and warden in areas **A6** and **A7**, respectively, should the need to return to the tomb arise after Haramil was interred. The tapestries were treated with *unguent of timelessness*, but even with this protection, their age is starting to show; they are brittle and unravel if handled. A PC who succeeds at a DC 15 Knowledge (religion) check determines that they depict aspects of Gozreh (the original patron of Haramil's clan before he turned his back on the gods to embrace the powers of the *Cradle of Night*). The tapestries depict Gozreh's fury against Haramil, and they serve as a promise of suffering in the afterlife for his faithlessness in life.

Creatures: A pair of powerful tomb guardians stand vigil in this room, ready to oppose any passing through other than worshippers of Gozreh. The western guardian appears as a statue of a fierce woman, while the eastern guardian appears as a statue of a stern, elderly man: these are both aspects of Gozreh, which the PCs can realize with successful DC 15 Knowledge (religion) checks. Each statue bears a metal trident clutched in its stony grip.

As soon as any creature enters this room, both guardians animate and turn to face the intruder. A *magic mouth* activates on each statue so that they speak in tandem in Hallit, the language of Haramil's tribe: "You tread upon corrupted ground. Turn back now, unless you come before us with the sacred sign of whispering wind and

Xermathiel

INTRODUCTION

CHAPTER 1:
REMNANTS OF THE DARK

CHAPTER 2:
GAME OF SHADOWS

CHAPTER 3:
FATE OF THE FORSAKEN

APPENDIX 1:
LYRUDRADA

APPENDIX 2:
BESTIARY

rippling waves in hand." If an intruder presents a holy symbol of Gozreh within 1 round of this proclamation, the guardians allow the symbol-bearer and her companions to pass through uncontested—otherwise, they attack.

TOMB GUARDIANS (2)	CR 7

XP 3,200 each

Advanced graven guardian of Gozreh (*Pathfinder RPG Bestiary 3* 290, 140)

N Medium construct

Init +2; **Senses** darkvision 60 ft., low-light vision; Perception +1

DEFENSE

AC 20, touch 12, flat-footed 18 (+2 Dex, +8 natural)

hp 75 each (10d10+20); fast healing 2

Fort +3, **Ref** +5, **Will** +4

DR 5/adamantine; **Immune** construct traits; **SR** 18

Weaknesses faith bound

OFFENSE

Speed 40 ft., fly 40 ft. (average)

Melee *+1 returning shock trident* +14/+9 (1d8+4 plus 1d6 electricity) or

slam +13 (1d6+4)

Ranged *+1 returning shock trident* +13 (1d8+3 plus 1d6 electricity)

Special Attacks magic weapon

Spell-Like Abilities (CL 10th; concentration +5)

1/day—*haste* (self only)

TACTICS

During Combat The tomb guardians each cast *haste* in the first round of combat. They thereafter each select separate targets to attack, if possible, to maximize their deterrence.

Morale The tomb guardians fight until destroyed, but they do not leave their hidden shrine.

STATISTICS

Str 16, **Dex** 15, **Con** —, **Int** —, **Wis** 12, **Cha** 1

Base Atk +10; **CMB** +13; **CMD** 25

Skills Fly +6; **Racial Modifiers** +4 Fly

SQ guardian domains (Air, Weather)

Gear mwk trident

A6. Trapped Corridor (CR 8)

Stone double doors stand at the north and south ends of this hallway. The east and west walls each have two niches just large enough to contain a human-sized statue of an armored warrior. Each of the statues is made of stone but also wears a real suit of hide armor and wields an elegant trident made of wood. The floor of the hallway is marred in two locations by ominous-looking circular scorch marks.

The north door leads to area **A7**, while the south door leads to area **A2**. There are two other secret exits from this room, each concealed behind one of the statues. A secret door to the hidden shrine (area **A5**) is behind the southeastern statue; a successful DC 25 Perception check is required to find it. This secret door is also locked, requiring a successful DC 25 Disable Device check to open. The other secret exit leads to the ruined hall (area **A8**); it also requires a successful DC 25 Perception check to find, although it isn't locked.

The statues themselves do not represent Haramil, although they are all male barbarians (which may cause some PCs to wonder if they in fact depict the warlord, until they see his spectral forms later on). These statues instead depict worshippers of Gozreh and are meant to represent the faithful standing guard against both tomb robbers looking to plunder the tomb and undead who rise from within it.

The scorch marks on the floor were left by the death throes of two dark slayers who were slain by the trap in this room when the Reborn infiltrated the tomb. A PC who succeeds at a DC 15 Perception or Survival check identifies a humanoid outline at the center of each of the scorch marks. Once these outlines are discovered, PCs can attempt a DC 14 Knowledge (local) check; on a success, a PC realizes that such scorch marks are all that remain of dark slayers who perish. If present, Aiyana automatically recognizes the scorches for what they are: proof that the Reborn have already visited the tomb.

Trap: This hallway features a complex magical trap meant to destroy both tomb robbers and any undead originating from within the tomb. The trap is armed when either the north or south doors are opened, and it triggers as soon as any Small or larger creature steps directly in front of any of the four statues. At that moment, two effects occur: first, all four statues jab forward with their tridents, which are momentarily imbued with magic to function as *+1 undead-bane ghost touch tridents*. Second, the north and south doors slam shut and lock with heavy metal bolts (Disable Device DC 30). On the following round, the floor of the hallway erupts into flames, as per a *wall of fire* (CL 10th), for 5 rounds. After that time, the *wall of fire* disappears and the doors unlock. The trap's magic takes 1 hour to recharge, at which point it automatically resets. If the armor and weapons are removed from all four statues, the trap is permanently deactivated.

CLEANSING CORRIDOR TRAP	CR 8

XP 4,800

Type magical; **Perception** DC 15 (if the scorch marks are removed, the Perception DC to notice this trap increases to 20); **Disable Device** DC 28

EFFECTS

Trigger visual (darkvision 60 ft.); **Reset** automatic (after 1 hour)

Effect Atk +10 melee (1d8+1 piercing), multiple targets (up to 4 creatures adjacent to the statues); spell effect (*wall of fire*, 2d4 fire damage to all creatures in area **A6** for 5 rounds)

Treasure: Each of the figures in the alcoves wears a suit of +1 *hide armor* and wields a +1 *trident*.

A7. Hungry Shadows (CR 8)

Stone double doors stand in the center of the south, east, and west walls of this room, although the door leading west is partially sealed with stone spread across the door like clay. A short pedestal bearing pale blue shards of shattered crystal occupies the center of this room, surrounded by a circle of runes carved into the floor. An alcove at the north end of this room contains a stone statue of a human man. The statue wields a lance and wears hide armor, but, strangely, it has been turned away from the center of the room to instead face the blank alcove wall to the north.

The pedestal once contained a potent magical lure designed to attract incorporeal undead and trap them within a crystal; the Reborn shattered the crystal as they passed through as part of their overall efforts to weaken any defenses in the tomb. Divining the room's true purpose—as well as the fact that the shattered crystal no longer functions as a trap—requires a successful DC 25 Knowledge (arcana or religion) check.

The statue to the north depicts Haramil; it was placed facing away from the room both to shame him, and due to ancient belief that the backward-facing statue of a deceased person would confuse the ambitions of his unquiet spirit. The PCs can recall this old superstition with a successful DC 25 Knowledge (history or religion) check.

The western door was sealed shut with a *stone shape* spell cast by one of the Reborn to seal the traitor Zyler within the ruined hall beyond (area **A8**). While the door's integrity has been compromised by the spell, it remains stuck fast and must be smashed open or broken to enter the room beyond (hardness 8, hp 40, break DC 22). The door to the south leads to the trapped corridor (area **A6**), and the door to the east leads to the false tomb (area **A9**).

Creature: When the Reborn stole the *Cradle of Night* and destroyed many of the tomb's wards, Haramil's long-lingering spirit split apart into three dangerous undead presences. One of those—a starving fragment of his hunger for power—manifested here as a greater shadow. The shadow lingers in the alcove around the statue, frustrated by the insult of the statue's positioning. The shadow appears as a black outline of the statue itself, and it surges forth to attack as soon as the PCs enter this room.

HARAMIL'S HUNGER	CR 8

XP 4,800

Greater shadow (*Pathfinder RPG Bestiary* 245)

hp 58

TACTICS

During Combat Haramil's hunger uses its Mobility and Flyby Attack feats to avoid being surrounded. It focuses its attacks

on foes using positive energy above all others; otherwise, it attacks whichever opponent most recently injured it. The shadow pursues foes throughout the tomb, but not beyond the tomb's limits.

Morale Haramil's hunger fights until destroyed.

Development: As long as at least one other fragment of Haramil's shattered soul (either Haramil's corruption or his madness) remains active, Haramil's hunger rejuvenates with full hit points in this room 24 hours after it is destroyed.

A8. Ruined Hall (CR 7)

The northern part of this long chamber has crumbled away into ruin, with rubble spilling onto the stone floor. A trickle of water filtering through cracks, the ceiling to the south has created a shallow rivulet and a wide pool in the middle of the room that drains slowly through the rubble to the north. The walls, crisscrossed with dozens of glistening slime trails left by pale gray slugs, depict a number of etchings of mounted warriors charging across a wide battlefield against one another, but the walls all bear signs of ancient damage.

The original architects of this chamber decorated this hall with images of Haramil's conquests before he succumbed to the curse of the *Cradle of Night*, then deliberately damaged the walls to symbolize the damage he had done to his legacy by falling under the artifact's influence. Water has been seeping through this room for only a few decades; in a few more years, erosion from the seepage will likely cause this chamber to collapse completely.

Creature: One of the more ambitious and self-serving members of the Reborn is a dark dancer named Zyler. He was among the group that infiltrated Haramil's tomb, but his reasons for doing so were selfish—he hoped to seize control of the band and claim the *Cradle of Night* for himself. Zyler's ambition was matched by his overconfidence, though, and the other Reborn discovered his treachery before he had a chance to seize the *Cradle of Night*. A deep-seated caligni superstition that a dark dancer's death is a bad omen was the only thing that kept the Reborn from executing Zyler on the spot. Instead, they overpowered him, threw him into this room, and sealed the door with a *stone shape* spell. The Reborn knew there was plenty of food (in the form of bitter-tasting slugs) and water (in the form of equally bitter runoff) to keep Zyler alive for some time—long enough time, the Reborn reasoned, to complete their plans and then return here to let the traitor loose and, in so doing, avoid the ill luck they fear his death would bring to their plots.

Zyler takes little comfort in being spared; although he's spent a relatively short time imprisoned here, he's already consumed by fantasies of violent vengeance against the Reborn. The desperate rogue uses his *wand of invisibility*

INTRODUCTION

**CHAPTER 1:
REMNANTS OF THE DARK**

**CHAPTER 2:
GAME OF SHADOWS**

**CHAPTER 3:
FATE OF THE FORSAKEN**

**APPENDIX 1:
LYRUDRADA**

**APPENDIX 2:
BESTIARY**

if he hears the telltale sound of someone trying to break through the door from area **A7**. When he realizes the intruders aren't fellow caligni, he becomes intrigued and watches for a few minutes to try to determine what the PCs are up to. If the PCs leave to explore other areas of the tomb, Zyler follows them from the shadows as quietly as possible.

If the PCs don't catch on to the fact that Zyler is spying on them, he continues to stalk them, becoming increasingly convinced that the PCs present his best opportunity for revenge, despite his generally low opinion of surface folk. As long as he remains unnoticed, Zyler does his best to aid the PCs when they need it but endeavors to remain unseen. If he remains undetected until the end of the adventure, he scuttles in and claims the *Cradle of Night* at the first opportunity, at which point destroying the PCs becomes his primary goal—see Concluding the Adventure for further details on this potential development.

If the PCs discover Zyler and confront him, the quick-thinking rogue relies first on his words rather than his weapons to further his plans (see the sidebar).

ZYLER	CR 7

XP 3,200

Male dark dancer rogue 6 (*Pathfinder RPG Bestiary 4* 43)

CE Small humanoid (dark folk)

Init +7; **Senses** see in darkness; Perception +14

DEFENSE

AC 19, touch 17, flat-footed 13 (+2 armor, +6 Dex, +1 size)

hp 74 (8d8+38)

Fort +6, **Ref** +16, **Will** +2

Defensive Abilities evasion, trap sense +2, uncanny dodge

Weaknesses light blindness

OFFENSE

Speed 30 ft.

Melee mwk short sword +14 (1d4/19–20 plus poison)

Ranged *+1 hand crossbow* +14 (1d3+1/19–20 plus poison)

Special Attacks bardic performance (8 rounds/day; distraction, inspire courage +1), dark curse, death throes, sneak attack +4d6

TACTICS

During Combat Zyler has no interest in fighting when outnumbered, and his primary goal in combat is to escape so that he can stalk the PCs and wait for the chance to claim the *Cradle of Night* for himself. If prevented from escaping, he relies on his *wand of blindness/deafness*. He uses lethal attacks against the PCs only as a last resort—he wants them to live long enough to carve him a path to the *Cradle of Night*.

Morale If reduced to fewer than 15 hit points, Zyler surrenders

An "Alliance" with Zyler

If the PCs end up talking with Zyler, the dark dancer does everything he can to convince them he's a valuable ally against the Reborn. He points out that the Reborn imprisoned him and uses that to convince the PCs he's on their side. Zyler's ability to help is limited by two things: his self-centeredness, and his lack of any real information about the cult. Zyler was hired by the Reborn to serve as a guide in navigating the strangeness of the surface world, as the dark dancer has served such a role several times before. Zyler saw the job as an opportunity to get into the good graces of an emerging power in Lyrudrada, but when he learned their goal, his plans shifted to treachery.

Zyler has no real knowledge of the Forsaken Fane or the structure of the Reborn cult, but he can provide the PCs with information about the various castes of caligni or the city of Lyrudrada (see Appendix 1 on page 56). He's not above using Bluff to tell the PCs what they want to hear, whether or not it's actually true, and he initially agrees to accompany them as a guide only to abandon them at the first opportunity so he can resume stalking them quietly and awaiting a chance to snatch the *Cradle of Night*.

Zyler and Aiyana don't know one another, but each is very suspicious of the other, and their bickering back and forth should be a strong clue that the dark dancer isn't to be trusted. If the PCs manage to establish Zyler's cooperation with magical control (such as *charm person*), he can become a more trustworthy ally, but his lack of any real knowledge about the Reborn and their plans should swiftly become apparent.

and begs for mercy as described in the An "Alliance" with Zyler sidebar above.

STATISTICS

Str 11, **Dex** 25, **Con** 16, **Int** 12, **Wis** 8, **Cha** 15

Base Atk +5; **CMB** +4; **CMD** 21

Feats Deadly Aim, Point-Blank Shot, Skill Focus (Use Magic Device), Toughness, Weapon Finesse

Skills Acrobatics +18, Bluff +13, Climb +4, Knowledge (geography) +8, Perception +14, Perform (dance) +13, Sleight of Hand +18, Stealth +26, Use Magic Device +16; **Racial Modifiers** +4 Climb, +4 Perception, +4 Stealth

Languages Common, Dark Folk

SQ poison use, rogue talents (fast stealth, finesse rogue), trapfinding +3

Combat Gear black smear poison (3 doses; *Pathfinder RPG Bestiary* 54), *wand of blindness/deafness* (15 charges), *wand of invisibility* (10 charges); **Other Gear** leather armor, mwk short sword, *+1 hand crossbow* with 20 bolts, *cloak of resistance +1*, 30 gp

A9. False Tomb (CR 8)

This large chamber's vaulted ceiling arches twenty feet overhead. Rich but aged tapestries hang from the walls along with several shields depicting a black circle upon a field of blue. Multiple life-sized statues occupy the edges of the main floor. Four represent armored warriors holding lances and two represent armored warhorses. To the east, a short flight of steps ascends to an alcove containing a stone coffin surrounded with weapons and other treasures. A long lance with a cruel barbed tip lies atop the coffin.

The tomb's architects feared that some of the more sinister allies Haramil acquired after his corruption might attempt to infiltrate the tomb to abscond with his body or the *Cradle of Night*, so they constructed this false crypt as an added protection. The chamber holds most of the warlord's possessions, including weapons and shields once borne by him in battle. The tapestries represent the heraldry he used at the height of his power, with the black orb representing the *Cradle of Night*; all have been preserved with *unguent of timelessness* but are now beginning to show their age.

Though the coffin in the eastern alcove is real, it contains only the remains of a soldier who fell in battle defending Haramil. A secret latch built into the coffin activates a hidden pulley with counterweights that lowers the entire platform down 20 feet to Haramil's true resting place in a subchamber below (area **A10**). Originally this latch was very well hidden, but damage to the area by the Reborn when they were searching for the *Cradle of Night* makes locating the latch much easier. Now, a PC needs only succeed at a DC 15 Perception check to locate the switch. The platform lowers gradually, reaching the floor of the subchamber below in 3 rounds. The counterweights automatically raise the platform back into position after 1 day.

The wall behind the southern horse statue contains a locked secret door to the hidden shrine (area **A5**), which requires a successful DC 25 Perception check to find and a successful DC 25 Disable Device check to unlock.

Creature: As in areas **A7** and **A10**, this chamber has become haunted by a portion of Haramil's fractured spirit. The manifestation in this tomb is of Haramil's corruption—everything that he once held dear twisted into foul putrefaction. When the PCs enter this room, this corruption appears as a unique, Large festering spirit rising up out of the coffin, picking up the lance atop the coffin as it does so. The spirit's connection to this lance

allows it to use its Dexterity score in place of its Strength score for both attack and damage rolls with the weapon. While the spirit appears as Haramil mounted on a horse, the undead creature is treated as a single being—it cannot be forced to dismount, for example, and it isn't treated as mounted for the purposes of dealing damage with its lance.

HARAMIL'S CORRUPTION	CR 9

XP 6,400
Variant festering spirit (*Pathfinder RPG Bestiary 4* 98)
CE Large undead (incorporeal)
Init +10; **Senses** darkvision 60 ft.; Perception +15
Aura stench (30 ft., DC 15, 10 rounds)

DEFENSE

AC 20, touch 20, flat-footed 13 (+4 deflection, +6 Dex, +1 dodge, −1 size)
hp 93 (11d8+44)
Fort +7, **Ref** +9, **Will** +8
Defensive Abilities channel resistance +2, incorporeal; **Immune** undead traits

OFFENSE

Speed fly 40 ft. (good)
Melee *+1 vicious lance* +15/+10 (1d8+10/×3 plus 2d6) or incorporeal touch +13 (1d4 Con plus slime)
Space 10 ft.; **Reach** 10 ft. (20 ft. with lance)
Special Attacks create spawn, slime, trample (1 Con plus slime, DC 19)

TACTICS

During Combat Haramil's corruption uses Flyby Attack each round as much as the close confines of the chamber allows. It focuses its attacks on large, heavily armored opponents when possible, as the corruption retains much of Haramil's pride and seeks to prove itself in battle against obviously mighty foes.
Morale Haramil's corruption fights until destroyed.

STATISTICS

Str —, **Dex** 22, **Con** —, **Int** 6, **Wis** 12, **Cha** 18
Base Atk +8; **CMB** +15; **CMD** 30
Feats Combat Reflexes, Dodge, Flyby Attack, Improved Initiative, Mobility, Weapon Focus (lance)
Skills Fly +8, Intimidate +9, Perception +15, Stealth +14
SQ ghost touch, undersized weapons
Gear Medium *+1 vicious lance*

Treasure: The Reborn were focused solely on acquiring the *Cradle of Night*, and so they ignored the other treasures here. In addition to the magic lance, many ancient valuables remain strewn about the coffin. These treasures include a masterwork composite shortbow (+4 Str), two masterwork daggers, a masterwork longsword, a masterwork spear, a masterwork trident, five bejeweled necklaces worth 250 gp each, three thick silver rings carved with stylized tree symbols worth 50 gp each, and three carved opals (depicting a mounted horselord, a rampaging hill giant, and a fire drake). Each of the opals is worth 800 gp.

Development: As long as at least one other fragment of Haramil's shattered soul (either his hunger or his madness) remains active, Haramil's corruption rejuvenates with full hit points in this room 24 hours after it is destroyed.

A10. Haramil's Crypt (CR 9)

Several stone pillars support the ceiling of this large chamber. Huge tapestries hang from every wall, each depicting landscapes and battles among hills and plains. A jet-black pedestal of carved rock stands empty to the north. Three scorched areas on the floor surround the crumbled remains of a stone statue to the south, near a closed stone coffin.

The coffin holds Haramil's actual remains, while the jet-black pedestal to the north once held the *Cradle of Night*. Apart from the third fragment of Haramil's fractured spirit (see Creature below), little remains for the PCs in this chamber other than confirmation that the *Cradle of Night* is missing. If she's with the party, Aiyana can confirm that the pedestal is perfectly sized to hold something of the *Cradle of Night's* dimensions. *Detect magic* and similar spells reveal a lingering aura of illusion [evil] magic on the pedestal, as well.

Haramil's stone coffin contains only the warlord's skeleton. He was buried in dishonor without any of his gear or armor, as a final insult to his legacy. Haramil's bones still bear the marks of the battle-wounds that ultimately killed him.

Creature: The third manifestation of Haramil's fractured spirit haunts this chamber. A roiling cloud of shadows and darkness surges up from his coffin to manifest as a caller in darkness. Each of the faces in this churning mass resembles Haramil's, which by this point should be easily recognizable from the numerous statues and carvings the PCs have seen throughout the tomb.

HARAMIL'S MADNESS	CR 9

XP 6,400
Caller in darkness (*Pathfinder RPG Bestiary 5* 48)
hp 97

TACTICS

During Combat Haramil's madness first casts *paranoia* on a melee combatant to disrupt the PCs' teamwork. It then casts *mind thrust V* or *greater oneiric horror* on other opponents to keep them occupied before closing to consume their minds with melee touch attacks.

Morale Haramil's madness fights until destroyed, but it cannot pursue foes into the upper chambers of the tomb.

Development: As long as at least one other fragment of Haramil's shattered soul (either his hunger or

Defeating Haramil

Although defeating the three fragments of Haramil's spirit is not required to seek out the Reborn and prevent their plot, putting the ancient horselord's soul to rest gives the PCs two additional rewards. Regardless of which of the three undead fragments is defeated last, when the final fragment is destroyed, a shuddering cry of relief echoes through the entire tomb. At the same moment, the shadowy influence over the tomb fades (although the shadowbound corruption afflicting the PCs remains in place).

Haramil's Blessing: After living for decades under the *Cradle of Night's* corruption and then lingering after death for many more centuries, Haramil's spirit is thankful to finally be freed to travel on to the Great Beyond. As his influence moves on, each PC feels the full extent of his gratitude. This affects each PC with a *heal* spell (CL 11th) and good fortune. The latter effect allows each PC to reroll any d20 roll once at any point in the future; the decision to use this reroll must be made immediately after learning whether the previous roll was a success or a failure, and the PC can use the better result.

Story Award: For putting Haramil's soul to rest and freeing him from the corruption that tarnished his legacy, award the PCs 9,600 XP.

his corruption) remains active, Haramil's madness rejuvenates with full hit points in this room 24 hours after it is destroyed.

Next Steps

Once it becomes obvious that the *Cradle of Night* has been taken from Haramil's tomb, Aiyana is disappointed, but that quickly gives way to fear and determination. She's convinced (correctly) that the Reborn have taken control of the artifact, and she wants to return to the city of Lyrudrada immediately to rejoin her allies and determine the next step in opposing the Reborn. And of course, she desperately wants the PCs to accompany her to help defend the city and prevent the Reborn from realizing their plans. She reiterates the fact that her allies will reward the PCs for their continued aid, but only if rescued from the Reborn's clutches.

As an additional incentive, Aiyana points out that shadows are a way of life in Lyrudrada, and the city has several experts in shadow magic who can help the PCs come to terms with their new shadowbound corruption.

While Aiyana is eager to proceed, she understands if the PCs want to take a few days to recover, resupply, and prepare for a journey into the Darklands city of Lyrudrada. When they're ready to go, continue with Chapter 2.

INTRODUCTION

CHAPTER 1:
REMNANTS OF THE DARK

CHAPTER 2:
GAME OF SHADOWS

CHAPTER 3:
FATE OF THE FORSAKEN

APPENDIX 1:
LYRUDRADA

APPENDIX 2:
BESTIARY

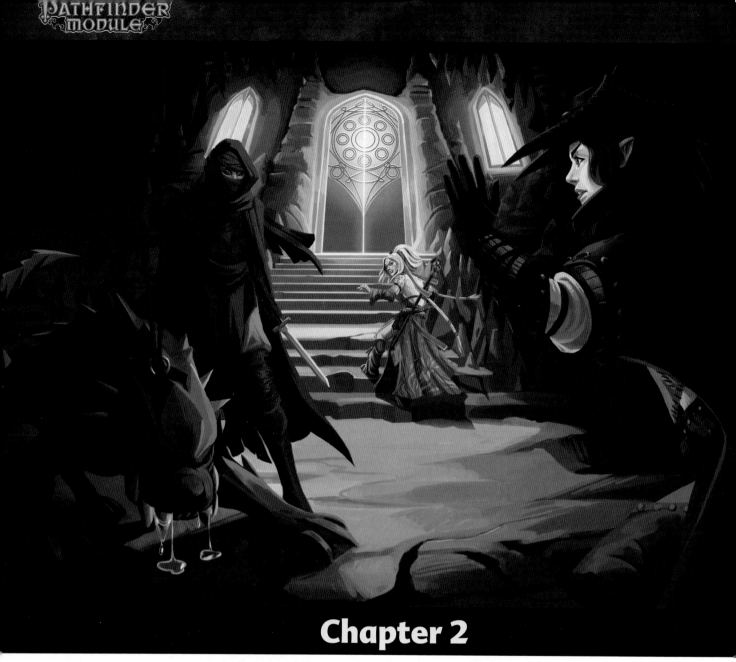

Chapter 2

Game Of Shadows

This adventure assumes that the PCs take up Aiyana's offer to travel to Lyrudrada safely and quickly via one of her *scrolls of shadow walk*. If the PCs prefer to make a more traditional journey, she grudgingly accepts their decision. *Pathfinder Campaign Setting: Into the Darklands* provides additional information about this dangerous region for PCs who choose to walk. The underground journey to Lyrudrada consists of an 85-mile trek through winding, relatively unused secondary tunnels of Nar-Voth (the uppermost layer of the Darklands). So long as Aiyana guides the party, they have no chance of hitting a dead end, becoming lost, or encountering an impassible verticality. Rules for travel in the Darklands can be found on page 10 of *Into the Darklands*, and tables for random wandering monsters

and random hazards can be found on the front inside cover and page 9, respectively, of that book. If you do not have access to *Into the Darklands* or prefer not to use it, feel free to augment the PCs' trip with wandering monsters or short encounters of your own design.

Aiyana knows that the Reborn are working quickly to gather power, and she's been gone from Lyrudrada long enough to warrant caution. She recommends that the PCs accompany her to her personal estate in Bleakshore to take stock of the situation and determine their next move.

Approaching Lyrudrada (CR 9)

Regardless of whether the PCs approach Lyrudrada with Aiyana's *shadow walk* spell or more mundane means, they encounter trouble shortly before arriving. The Reborn

INTRODUCTION

CHAPTER 1:
REMNANTS OF THE DARK

CHAPTER 2:
GAME OF SHADOWS

CHAPTER 3:
FATE OF THE FORSAKEN

APPENDIX 1:
LYRUDRADA

APPENDIX 2:
BESTIARY

have learned of the secret Bleakshore Council working against them and have captured many of the council's members. The Reborn also know of Aiyana's mission to recruit uplander aid and want to prevent Aiyana and the PCs from ever reaching Lyrudrada. They dispatched the umbral dragon Thelamistos (area **F9**) and four shadow mastiffs to hunt down Aiyana and her new allies. Thelamistos doesn't intend to confront Aiyana and the PCs just yet—as he wants to gauge their potential as a threat—but the hounds are eager for blood.

Creatures: Two shadow mastiffs patrol the Shadow Plane approach to Lyrudrada while the other pair stalks the Material Plane tunnels. No matter how the PCs approach the city, they are spotted by one pair, which makes their presence known by unleashing an eerie baying howl that echoes across the boundary between the two planes. The mastiffs on the same plane as the PCs attack 1 round later, with the other group lying in wait to ambush the PCs should they jump between planes— perhaps even stalking the PCs into the city once they arrive at their destination.

SHADOW MASTIFFS (4)   **CR 5**
XP 1,600 each
hp 51 each (*Pathfinder RPG Bestiary 3* 241)

Development: At the end of the battle, any PC who succeeds at a DC 26 Perception check spots Thelamistos spying on them from a distance and quickly departing. If on the Material Plane, PCs who succeed at the check catch a gleam of malevolent red eyes retreating in the distance, followed by the sound of scales scraping on stone. If on the Shadow Plane, successful PCs catch a glimpse of a great draconic shadow receding to the sound of beating wings. In either case, the PCs shouldn't catch Thelamistos at this time.

B. AIYANA'S ESTATE

Lyrudrada has seen major changes in Aiyana's absence. The Reborn have gained some measure of authority over the anarchic city and are working to strengthen their control. The Reborn discovered the existence of the Bleakshore Council working against them, rounded up its members, and commandeered Aiyana's estate as their base of operations while they hunt down other enemies. Aiyana quickly learns this information from sympathetic citizens of Bleakshore on the way to her estate, and she asks the PCs' help to recover her home.

The leader of the Reborn forces at Aiyana's estate is a dark dancer bard named Callivarius, a foolish but influential member of a prominent family in the Stalker's Reach district. The umbral dragon Thelamistos has reported Aiyana's return to Veilisendri and Nephenie in the Forsaken Fane, but these leaders haven't yet determined how best to respond; the PCs therefore have

a small window of opportunity to reclaim Aiyana's estate before Callivarius hears they've come to Lyrudrada.

Callivarius set up exterior patrols around the estate, but in her overconfidence she believes that the Bleakshore Council has been crushed and that the estate is easily defended. Although members of the Reborn at the estate are diligent in defending the structure, they don't feel any particular loyalty to the foppish aristocrat. Callivarius is unaware of the secret rear entrance to the estate (area **B20**), which could prove her undoing.

Aiyana's estate is location **2** on the Lyrudrada poster map, and a map of the estate itself is on the reverse of that poster map. When the PCs approach the estate, they can see the Reborn forces patrolling the area (area **B1**) before they are close enough to be seen. Aiyana recommends entry through the secret postern to catch the Reborn forces by surprise, but she defers to the party's decision in the matter. In any case, she is intimately familiar with the layout of her lifelong home, so the PCs can reference the estate poster map as long as Aiyana is present.

The estate consists of a cluster of stalagmites that have grown together over eons, hollowed out into comfortable and spacious chambers. The walls and floors are made of smooth stone, and ceilings are 15 feet high and vaulted unless otherwise noted. The doors are of hardened fungal planks and have the consistency and durability of strong wood (hardness 5, hp 20, break DC 25). The doors can all be locked (Disable Device DC 25), but only those indicated are locked at this time. Aiyana and Callivarius both hold master keys that unlock all doors in the estate. Aiyana is the only daughter of a wealthy line of caligni merchants, so her home is finely appointed with rich carpets, luxurious furniture, and vibrant frescoes, though Aiyana takes a dim view of any PCs who seek to loot her home. None of the rooms have light sources.

B1. Estate Approach (CR 8 or 10)

A cluster of large stalagmites has grown together here into a miniature multi-peaked mountain. Artistic glimmers of magical light highlight aesthetically pleasing shapes and colorful formations on the rocky prominence. Great doors of silver-chased, ebony-colored planks provide entry at the base of the structure.

Aiyana knows the front doors to her estate well, but she suggests using the secret door (area **B20**) instead. This secret door normally requires a successful DC 30 Perception check to find and is locked, but Aiyana knows where it is and has a key.

Creatures: Two patrols monitor the estate exterior, each consisting of a Reborn commando and a trained shadow mastiff (the commandos are unaffected by the mastiffs' baying). One patrol remains by the front doors at all times while the other circles the estate, checking in

with the patrol at the front doors every 5 minutes. In the event of attack, the shadow mastiffs bay to alert the other patrol, which arrives as soon as possible. Although the baying isn't normally loud enough to alert anyone within the estate, a commando near the front doors during an attack opens it so the sounds of combat alert the Reborn in area **B2** to intruders.

REBORN COMMANDOS (2)   CR 7

XP 3,200 each

Dark stalker ranger 3 (*Pathfinder RPG Bestiary* 54)

NE Medium humanoid (dark folk)

Init +5; **Senses** see in darkness; Perception +13

DEFENSE

AC 21, touch 15, flat-footed 16 (+4 armor, +5 Dex, +2 natural)

hp 91 each (9 HD; 6d8+3d10+48)

Fort +9, **Ref** +13, **Will** +6

Weaknesses light blindness

OFFENSE

Speed 30 ft.

Melee *+1 short sword* +11/+11/+6 (1d6+5/19–20)

Special Attacks combat style (two-weapon combat), death throes, favored enemy (dark folk +2), sneak attack +3d6

Spell-Like Abilities (CL 6th; concentration +6)

At will—*deeper darkness, detect magic, fog cloud*

TACTICS

During Combat A Reborn commando attempts to flank an opponent when possible, but casts *deeper darkness* to gain a good position for sneak attacks if fighting alone.

Morale A Reborn commando is a fanatic and fights to the death, confident in the immortality promised by Nephenie and Veilisendri.

STATISTICS

Str 18, **Dex** 20, **Con** 19, **Int** 9, **Wis** 13, **Cha** 11

Base Atk +7; **CMB** +11; **CMD** 26

Feats Double Slice, Endurance, Iron Will, Quick Draw, Toughness, Two-Weapon Fighting, Weapon Focus (short sword)

Skills Climb +12, Intimidate +8, Perception +13, Stealth +17, Survival +9; **Racial Modifiers** +4 Climb, +4 Perception, +4 Stealth

Languages Dark Folk, Undercommon

SQ favored terrain (underground +2), poison use, track +1, wild empathy +3

Combat Gear *potion of cure light wounds*, black smear poison (2 doses; *Pathfinder RPG Bestiary* 54); **Other Gear** *+1 studded leather*, *+1 short swords* (2), 5 gp

---

SHADOW MASTIFFS (2)   CR 5

XP 1,600 each

hp 51 each (*Pathfinder RPG Bestiary 3* 241)

B2. Main Hall (CR 10)

This large hall is richly decorated with murals, decorative tapestries, marble columns, and a high seat carved of jade-green stone. Two statues carved to resemble tall dark folk encased in full armor with open-faced great helms flank the grand entrance. The floor contains intricate mosaics showing underground scenes of triumphant dark folk armies, strange subterranean beasts, surface folk being led in chains, and shadowy gods looking on from above.

Built by Aiyana's grandfather, this hall depicts an idealized version of her family's lineage. The statues represent dark champions (see page 60), several of which have blessed the family's ranks over the years, and the mosaics depict mythologized versions of caligni history. Aiyana hasn't altered any of this decor, although she takes no real pleasure in it and is embarrassed by the depictions if the PCs investigate them closely.

Creatures: A Reborn officer currently sits in the great seat here, receiving reports from two Reborn commandos. If aware of intruders, the officer orders the commandos to hold this chamber while she releases the shadow mastiffs from the dining hall (area **B11**).

REBORN OFFICER   CR 7

XP 3,200

Dark creeper fighter 5 (*Pathfinder RPG Bestiary* 53)

CN Small humanoid (dark folk)

Init +4; **Senses** see in darkness; Perception +11

DEFENSE

AC 20, touch 15, flat-footed 16 (+5 armor, +4 Dex, +1 size)

hp 85 (8 HD; 3d8+5d10+45)

Fort +9, **Ref** +8, **Will** +5 (+1 vs. fear)

Weaknesses light blindness

OFFENSE

Speed 20 ft.

Melee *+1 heavy pick* +14/+9 (1d4+8/×4 plus poison)

Ranged mwk composite longbow +13/+8 (1d6+3/×3)

Special Attacks death throes, sneak attack +1d6, weapon training (axes +1)

Spell-Like Abilities (CL 3rd; concentration +3)

At will—*darkness, detect magic*

TACTICS

During Combat The officer drinks a *potion of rage* and confronts the toughest-looking opponent.

Morale The officer retreats to find reinforcements if reduced to fewer than 50 hit points, but if no reinforcements are nearby, the officer fights to the death against enemies of the Reborn.

STATISTICS

Str 16, **Dex** 18, **Con** 18, **Int** 7, **Wis** 12, **Cha** 10

Base Atk +7; **CMB** +9; **CMD** 23

Feats Iron Will, Point-Blank Shot, Power Attack, Precise Shot, Toughness, Weapon Focus (heavy pick), Weapon Specialization (heavy pick)

Skills Climb +9, Perception +11, Stealth +11; **Racial Modifiers** +4 Climb, +4 Perception, +4 Stealth

Languages Dark Folk

INTRODUCTION

CHAPTER 1:
REMNANTS OF THE DARK

CHAPTER 2:
GAME OF SHADOWS

CHAPTER 3:
FATE OF THE FORSAKEN

APPENDIX 1:
LYRUDRADA

APPENDIX 2:
BESTIARY

SQ armor training 1, poison use, rag armor
Combat Gear *potion of cure moderate wounds, potions of
rage* (2), black smear poison (3 doses; *Pathfinder RPG
Bestiary* 54); **Other Gear** *+1 hide armor, +1 heavy pick*,
mwk composite longbow (+3 Str) with 20 arrows, 27 gp

REBORN COMMANDOS (2)	CR 7

XP 3,200 each
hp 91 each (see page 22)

Treasure: The great seat is composed of a greenish
stone inset with 25 large pieces of jade worth 80 gp each.

Development: Combat here alerts the Reborn in areas
B7 and **B12**, who arrive in 1d4+2 rounds.

B3. Kitchen

Once a fine kitchen, this room is in shambles. Crockery and
utensils have been broken or discarded haphazardly, and the
spoiled remains of many meals lie strewn about.

Once used for the preparation of fine meals by Aiyana's
personal cook, this room has been well plundered by
the Reborn. A thorough inventory reveals that all of
Aiyana's personal staples have been consumed, and the
various bins and cabinets now hold the Reborn's rough,
low-quality rations in sufficient quantity to feed the
occupants of the estate for another 2 weeks.

B4. Cook's Room

A single bed occupies this chamber next to an open footlocker
of carved dark wood. The contents of the locker and the
bedclothes themselves lie strewn about the room.

This room, once the quarters of Aiyana's
personal cook, has been serving as the
quarters of one of the Reborn commandos
currently on patrol in area **B1**.

Treasure: The mahogany footlocker is worth 25
gp, but it is worth twice this much to dwellers
of the Darklands, where wood is scarce.

B5. Butler's Room

A bed occupies the far wall of this chamber next to a breakfront
cabinet of metal and fungal planks. A low shelf set into the
cabinet holds a still-intact porcelain bowl and the shattered
remains of a glass vase. A small wall niche holds the broken
remains of a piece of fine statuary which, based on the
chipping of nearby stone and broken crossbow bolts nearby,
was recently used as target practice.

This chamber was once the abode of Aiyana's butler,
though he was slain when the Reborn attacked. It is now

used by one of the two Reborn commandos currently on
patrol in area **B1**. The breakfront cabinet had held the
butler's attire and a few books, but these have since been
looted. A secret door stands at the rear of the statuary
niche. It was once difficult to find, but the recent damage
to the stone in the niche means it can be found with a
successful DC 19 Perception check.

Treasure: The porcelain bowl is finely crafted and
etched in gold; it is worth 70 gp. Another mahogany trunk
worth 25 gp, matching the one in area **B4**, is tucked under
the bed here and requires a successful DC 15 Perception
check to locate. The chest holds some valuables gathered
by the room's current occupant: 37 gp, 128 sp, an agate
worth 170 gp, a masterwork repeating heavy crossbow,
and a *potion of lesser restoration*.

B6. Butler's Pantry (CR 7)
This secret pantry has not been discovered by the estate's
current occupants. The butler used this pantry as both a
wine cellar and a location to hide his own valuables. The
pantry contains a small wine rack, two large clay jars with
lids, and a small chest of fungal planks.

Reborn Officer

Creature: The butler was not above a certain level of paranoia and left a guardian of sorts to protect his stash. One of the clay jars has been weakened so that if it is opened or jostled, it breaks open to dump out its contents: a compressed mass of rot grubs that immediately expands into a swarm. A PC who succeeds at a DC 30 Perception check notes the fragility of the jar. The butler had fed these rot grubs by carefully dropping table scraps into the jar, but the rot grubs have gone so long without food that they are now voraciously hungry.

ROT GRUB SWARM	CR 7

XP 3,200

hp 85 (*Pathfinder RPG Bestiary 3* 215)

Treasure: The wine rack holds five bottles of fine drow wine worth 40 gp each. The wooden chest contains 20 gp, 24 pp, a *potion of fly*, a *ring of climbing*, a *scroll of daybreak arrow*^{UC}, and a *wand of daylight* (23 charges). The clay jar that doesn't contain the rot grubs holds a *potion of ablative barrier*^{UC} and 20 smoke pellets^{UE}.

B7. Servants' Common Room (CR 9)

This chamber contains a round table and several chairs. Shelves on the west wall hold books, games, mugs, and casks. Several blankets are strewn across the floor amid a great deal of rubbish. Doors stand in each wall.

This room was once set aside as a place for the estate's servants to relax and entertain themselves in their downtime; the current occupants use it for essentially the same purpose. The doors to the north and west lead to the main hall (area **B2**), while the other doors lead to chambers set aside for some of the estate's other servants.

Creatures: Two Reborn cutthroats seated at the table here play dominoes and drink jacks of sour caligni beer. They may be encountered elsewhere, responding to alarms from elsewhere in the estate, but if encountered here, they immediately attack.

REBORN CUTTHROATS (2)	CR 7

XP 3,200 each

Dark creeper rogue 5 (*Pathfinder RPG Bestiary* 53)

CN Small humanoid (dark folk)

Init +5; **Senses** see in darkness; Perception +10

DEFENSE

AC 20, touch 17, flat-footed 14 (+2 armor, +5 Dex, +1 dodge, +1 natural, +1 size)

hp 81 each (8d8+45)

Fort +6, **Ref** +12, **Will** +2

Defensive Abilities evasion, trap sense +1, uncanny dodge

Weaknesses light blindness

OFFENSE

Speed 30 ft.

Melee *+1 short sword* +12 (1d4+3/19–20 plus poison)

Ranged mwk hand crossbow +12 (1d3/19–20 plus poison)

Special Attacks death throes, sneak attack +4d6 plus 4 bleed

Spell-Like Abilities (CL 3rd; concentration +1)

At will—*darkness, detect magic*

TACTICS

Before Combat Reborn cutthroats attempt to use their *elixir of hiding* before combat to gain an advantageous position.

During Combat Reborn cutthroats cast *darkness* to confuse the field of battle and attempt to make sneak attacks from hiding. If unable to hide, they try to flank opponents.

Morale Reborn cutthroats are fanatical but clever. After taking more than 20 points of damage, a cutthroat retreats to consume another *elixir of hiding* before rejoining the fight.

STATISTICS

Str 15, **Dex** 20, **Con** 18, **Int** 10, **Wis** 10, **Cha** 6

Base Atk +5; **CMB** +6; **CMD** 22

Feats Dodge, Mobility, Toughness, Weapon Finesse

Skills Acrobatics +16, Bluff +9, Climb +11, Disable Device +14, Escape Artist +16, Knowledge (dungeoneering) +7, Knowledge (local) +7, Perception +10, Sense Motive +5, Sleight of Hand +13, Stealth +24; **Racial Modifiers** +4 Climb, +4 Perception, +4 Stealth

Languages Dark Folk

SQ poison use, rag armor, rogue talents (bleeding attack, surprise attack), trapfinding +2

Combat Gear *elixirs of hiding* (2), *potions of cure moderate wounds* (2), black smear poison (4 doses; *Pathfinder RPG Bestiary* 54); **Other Gear** *+1 short sword*, mwk hand crossbow with 20 bolts, *amulet of natural armor +1*, mwk thieves' tools, 90 gp

Treasure: The dark creepers are playing with a set of onyx dominoes with tiny inset pearl pips, worth 175 gp for the set. Piled on the table are another 27 gp in bets.

Development: A fight here wakes the cutthroat in area **B8** in 1d3 rounds, who drinks his *elixir of hiding* and comes to investigate.

B8. Servants' Quarters (CR 7)

Three beds occupy this filthy, debris-strewn chamber. A cabinet stands across from the bed, its doors open and its contents pulled out onto the floor.

Formerly the quarters for the general servants of the estate, this room is occupied by Reborn cutthroats.

Creature: Unless awoken by an alarm or combat in area **B7**, a single Reborn cutthroat is asleep in the southernmost bed in this chamber. If awakened, he gathers his weapons and rushes into combat.

REBORN CUTTHROAT	CR 7

XP 3,200

hp 81 (see above)

INTRODUCTION

CHAPTER 1:
REMNANTS OF THE DARK

CHAPTER 2:
GAME OF SHADOWS

CHAPTER 3:
FATE OF THE FORSAKEN

APPENDIX 1:
LYRUDRADA

APPENDIX 2:
BESTIARY

B9. Chamberlain's Quarters

A single bed and nightstand rest against the curved southeast wall of the room. A row of hooks on the west wall contains several rags in bunched disarray.

The Reborn officer currently occupying this room, formerly the estate chamberlain's quarters, has attempted to adopt the previous resident's cultured airs. However, since dark creepers are generally unfamiliar with the concept of not wearing every owned article of clothing at all times, the effect has been less than successful.

Treasure: The drawer to the nightstand is jammed shut; opening it requires a successful DC 15 Disable Device or Strength check. Inside are two vials of padzahr[UE] and a neatly folded courtier's outfit sized for a Medium creature.

B10. Storage

This storeroom has been ransacked and used as a privy, based on the eye-watering stench and obvious stains.

B11. Dining Hall (CR 8)

Once a spacious dining hall, this room has been converted into a kennel. Two once-fine tables and an assortment of chairs and benches have been turned into gnawed wrecks. The tapestries and banners that once adorned the walls have been torn down and left in tangled piles. A statue in one corner depicts a dark stalker of noble bearing but bears many scratches and stains.

The furnishings in this chamber have been utterly destroyed by the occupants, and the statue depicting one of Aiyana's famous ancestors is ruined.

Creatures: The Reborn use this chamber as a kennel for their pack of five shadow mastiffs used to guard the estate. Three of the beasts are currently here, while the other two patrol area **B1**. The shadow mastiffs don't generally respond to attacks on the estate unless a member of the Reborn comes and gets them.

SHADOW MASTIFFS (3)	CR 5

XP 1,600 each
hp 51 each (*Pathfinder RPG Bestiary 3* 241)

Treasure: Among the gnawed bones and leavings of the mastiffs' meals is a bezoar that one of the mastiffs developed after eating a xorn. Mixed with the hair and hardened mud of this gut-stone are dozens of small carnelians worth a total of 165 gp. The PCs can locate these gemstones with a successful DC 31 Perception check.

Development: The shadow mastiff's baying can be heard anywhere within the estate, which awakens and alerts all the estate's current residents. A fight here draws the occupants of area **B2** in 1d3+1 rounds.

B12. Guard Quarters (CR 7)

This chamber is austere, holding only three bunks and their adjacent footlockers.

Aiyana's personal hired guards once occupied this chamber, though all were killed in the Reborn raid. One of the bunks still bears singed bedclothes from where the caligni guard was murdered in her sleep.

Creature: Three Reborn commandos are quartered in here, though two of them are currently reporting to their officer in area **B2**. The third commando is resting on his bunk and reading from a scroll of terrible dark folk poetry called *The Ode to the Owb*. If caught unawares, this commando casts *deeper darkness* to provide cover and attempts to alert the occupants of areas **B2** and **B13** before entering melee.

REBORN COMMANDO	CR 7

XP 3,200
hp 91 (see page 22)

Treasure: Each of the footlockers holds a haphazard assortment of well-used whetstones, spare boots, a few saved rations, and other odds and ends, including a total of 13 gp and a bloodstone worth 80 gp.

Development: Loud noises here wake the occupants of area **B13** in 1d3 rounds.

B13. Armory (CR 9)

An empty weapons rack stands against the east wall, with two messy cots next to it.

Once the estate's armory, this chamber was looted after the estate was taken, leaving nothing of value behind.

Creatures: This room has been converted into quarters for two Reborn commandos, currently sleeping upon the cots. They awaken to the sounds of combat in adjacent rooms and grab their weapons without taking time to put on their armor.

UNARMORED REBORN COMMANDOS (2)	CR 7

XP 3,200 each
AC 17, touch 15, flat-footed 12 (+5 Dex, +2 natural)
hp 91 each (see page 22)

Treasure: Two suits of +1 *studded leather* are stuffed under the cots; they belong to the commandos that are sleeping here.

B14. Trophy Hall (CR 7)

The walls of this chamber are hung with all manner of banners, weapons, trinkets, and bits of armor, as well as

more than a few stuffed and mounted examples of Darklands creatures. Two statues adorn the corners of the chamber. One depicts a noble-looking caligni wrapped in chains, and the other a decapitated duergar holding its startled head in its hands. The once-polished tile floor is now marred by many muddy tracks.

This was the trophy hall of Aiyana's family. Relics here include a broken rhoka sword from the warlike urdefhan race and a centuries-old Chelish legionnaire's helm from the Shadow Caverns massacre. The statue of the chain-covered caligni depicts one of Aiyana's distant ancestors, who was rumored to bear kyton blood. If specifically asked about the duergar statue, Aiyana is startled to realize she has never seen it before. Its plinth had formerly been occupied by the bust of her grandfather, but the bust is now missing.

The tracks on the floor appear to be a combination of dried mud and some sort of greasy substance, which a PC can identify as slurk slime if she succeeds at a DC 17 Knowledge (arcana) check. The tracks were left by Callivarius's dark creeper valets as they travel back and forth between Callivarius's quarters and the laundry.

Creature: The bust of Aiyana's grandfather reminded Callivarius of a cephalophore in her own estate, so she had the bust removed and brought the cephalophore as additional security. It now stands guard here and attacks anyone not accompanied by Callivarius or one of her dark creeper valets. The construct isn't used to its new, busier surroundings, so it requires 1d3 rounds to realize that the PCs aren't authorized. The cephalophore begins combat with its dazing gaze before stepping forward to make slam attacks, at which point it fights until destroyed. The construct is life-sized for a duergar; the young simple template reflects its smaller-than-normal size for a cephalophore.

YOUNG CEPHALOPHORE CR 7
XP 3,200
hp 86 (*Pathfinder RPG Bestiary 4* 289, 27)

B15. Guest Quarters (CR 8)

Unlike the rest of the estate, this room appears to be undisturbed. There are four well-made beds, a table with seating for six, and a sideboard bearing a silver pitcher and basin. A finely painted mural on the ceiling depicts a subterranean river descending into a swirling whirlpool where Darklands fey and aquatic creatures cavort.

This guest chamber is largely intact, though the Reborn cutthroats set a trap as a malicious prank.

Trap: The silver pitcher is half-filled with a very weak acid (no damage). However, delicately balanced in the neck of the pitcher is a sponge soaked in concentrated

insanity mist and allowed to dry. Handling the pitcher causes the sponge to drop into the acid and immediately release a cloud of insanity mist that fills the entire room. The insanity mist disperses after 3 rounds.

INSANITY MIST TRAP CR 8
XP 4,800
Type mechanical; **Perception** DC 25; **Disable Device** DC 20
EFFECTS
Trigger touch; **Reset** none
Effect poison gas (insanity mist), never miss, onset delay (1 round), multiple targets (all targets in area **B15**)

Treasure: The silver pitcher and basin are worth 160 gp together, though they have been in Aiyana's family for many years and she isn't inclined to part with them.

B16. Laundry and Lavatory (CR 6)

Tubs and tables made of pale fungal planks stand against the walls of this room. At the north end of the room, a large stone tub squats in its own alcove. A cast-iron stove stands nearby with an attached bucket for heating water. A thick layer of slimy mud covers the floor and the bottom several feet of the walls around the room.

This room is the estate's laundry and bath, with a lavatory in an alcove around the corner. The estate's occupiers aren't much interested in doing laundry, but have nevertheless found a use for the chamber's tub.

Creatures: Callivarius's most prized possession is an enormous pet slurk named Sudor. The slime-covered creature is pampered by the dark dancer's personal valets, who bring it here from its lair in area **B17** several times a day to soak in the tub. Sudor is currently wedged in the tub while two valets scrub it with damp towels. If interrupted, the valets immediately draw daggers to defend their master's prized pet, while Sudor takes 1 round to extricate itself from the tub (during which time it is treated as entangled) before leaping into combat. These foes try to flee if reduced to fewer than 10 hit points; Sudor eagerly overruns foes in its haste to escape.

DARK CREEPERS (2) CR 2
XP 600 each
hp 19 each (*Pathfinder RPG Bestiary* 53)

SUDOR CR 4
XP 1,200
Advanced giant slurk
hp 25 (*Pathfinder RPG Bestiary 2* 292, 293, 251)

Development: Although the occupants of this room aren't likely to pose much challenge to the PCs, the noise of combat here wakens the commandos in area **B13**.

INTRODUCTION

CHAPTER 1:
REMNANTS OF THE DARK

CHAPTER 2:
GAME OF SHADOWS

CHAPTER 3:
FATE OF THE FORSAKEN

APPENDIX 1:
LYRUDRADA

APPENDIX 2:
BESTIARY

B17. Storage

The shelves of this storage chamber have been stripped bare, their contents smashed and mixed into a slimy morass on the floor to create a large, soggy nest. The walls of the chamber are likewise covered in foul slime.

Callivarius looted this storeroom and then converted it into a lair for her enormous pet slurk, Sudor. It is currently unoccupied while Callivarius's valets give Sudor his bath.

B18. Master Lounge (CR 5)

This comfortably appointed lounge has a large stone fireplace, though its ashes are currently cold. Opposite the fireplace is a comfortable sofa upholstered in some kind of fuzzy hide. A number of rag piles that appear to serve as bed rolls are scattered throughout the room, and the malodorous stench of unwashed bodies is heavy in the air.

Creatures: This chamber has been taken over by Callivarius's entourage of dark creeper valets. Five of these creatures reside here, though only three are currently present (the other two are washing the slurk in area **B16**). These valets are neither warriors nor Reborn true believers; they attempt to flee if injured at all.

DARK CREEPERS (3)	CR 2

XP 600 each
hp 19 each (*Pathfinder RPG Bestiary* 53)

Treasure: The rich furnishings in this chamber are worth a total of 3,000 gp, but belong to Aiyana.

B19. Master Bedroom (CR 10)

The doors to this chamber are kept locked; only Callivarius and Aiyana have keys.

This opulent bedroom contains two beds, each bearing ornately carved wooden headboards, which are rare and valuable in a subterranean city. Two nightstands, one bearing a chamber pot and the other bearing a silver tea service, stand beside the beds. The floor is covered in a thick, shaggy rug of brightly colored geometric designs, and the domed ceiling is painted with a mural that resembles a starry night sky—another luxury in a city that has never seen such a sight.

Aiyana took over this bedchamber after the deaths of her parents several years ago, though she never replaced their separate beds out of a sense of nostalgia. The secret door requires a successful DC 30 Perception check to locate; Callivarius is unaware it exists.

Creatures: The Reborn sent a dark dancer aristocrat named Callivarius to lead the attack on Aiyana's estate. She only recently joined the Reborn, but as she comes

from a prominent family in the Stalker's Reach district, she was immediately afforded a high rank within the cult. Although the attack on the estate was successful, the Reborn who report to her don't like her, accurately considering her a dandy who prefers to be surrounded by servants and pampered pets rather than devout fanatics. Nevertheless, Callivarius is determined to prove her worth to the Reborn by killing or capturing Aiyana and the PCs.

CALLIVARIUS	CR 10

XP 9,600
Female dark dancer bard 9 (*Pathfinder RPG Bestiary 4* 43)
CN Small humanoid (dark folk)
Init +9; **Senses** see in darkness; Perception +11

DEFENSE

AC 24, touch 17, flat-footed 18 (+5 armor, +5 Dex, +1 dodge, +2 shield, +1 size)
hp 113 (11d8+64)
Fort +8, **Ref** +15, **Will** +8; +4 vs. bardic performance, language-dependent, and sonic
Weaknesses light blindness

OFFENSE

Speed 30 ft.
Melee *+1 spell storing rapier* +14/+9 (1d4+3/18–20)
Special Attacks bardic performance 24 rounds/day (move action; countersong, dirge of doom, distraction, fascinate [DC 18], inspire competence +3, inspire courage +3, inspire greatness, *suggestion* [DC 18]), dark curse, death throes, sneak attack +1d6
Bard Spells Known (CL 9th; concentration +13)
3rd (4/day)—*charm monster* (DC 17), *cure serious wounds, haste, slow* (DC 17)
2nd (5/day)—*hold person* (DC 16), *mirror image, sound burst* (DC 16), *suggestion* (DC 16)
1st (6/day)—*charm person* (DC 15), *cure light wounds, disguise self, saving finale*^APG (DC 15), *vanish*^APG
0 (at will)—*detect magic, ghost sound* (DC 14), *mage hand, message, prestidigitation, resistance*

TACTICS

Before Combat Callivarius tries to use *charm monster* and *suggestion* to avoid battle altogether.
During Combat Once battle is joined, Callivarius casts *haste* and attempts to incapacitate foes by using dirge of doom followed by *hold person*.
Morale Callivarius is loyal to the Reborn but far from foolhardy. If reduced below 20 hit points, she casts *vanish* and attempts to escape.

STATISTICS

Str 14, **Dex** 21, **Con** 18, **Int** 8, **Wis** 8, **Cha** 18
Base Atk +7; **CMB** +8; **CMD** 24
Feats Arcane Strike, Dodge, Improved Initiative, Iron Will, Toughness, Weapon Finesse
Skills Bluff +12, Climb +6, Intimidate +12, Perception +11, Perform (dance, oratory) +18, Sleight of Hand +13, Stealth +21; **Racial Modifiers** +4 Climb, +4 Perception, +4 Stealth

Languages Dark Folk
SQ bardic knowledge +4, lore master 1/day, poison use,
versatile performances (dance, oratory)
Gear *+1 mithral chain shirt, +1 buckler, +1 spell storing rapier*
(contains *hold person*), *cloak of resistance +1*, key to doors
in Aiyana's estate, 17 pp, 5 gp

Development: If Callivarius escapes, she makes her way
back to the Forsaken Fane to report on Aiyana and the
PCs. In this event, Callivarius joins the assassination team
sent after Shevarimarr and the PCs to try to salvage her
reputation with the Reborn (see page 33).

Callivarius

B20. Postern (CR 3)
Both secret doors to this chamber are difficult to find
(Perception DC 30 to locate) and are locked (Disable
Device DC 30).

This small chamber is dusty and cramped. A narrow alcove
contains a large barrel with a small knapsack atop it, a blanket,
and a clean bucket.

Aiyana's great-grandfather installed this chamber as a
bolt-hole, insurance against the threat of an insurrection
in the city, and Aiyana regularly refreshes its contents
for emergencies. The cask holds fresh water, and the
knapsack holds nourishing but unpalatable rations.

Creature: A necrophidius stretches across the lintel of
the northern secret door, prepared to slither down to fight
anyone other than Aiyana or creatures accompanying her.
Aiyana calls the necrophidius Tickles, and it follows her
commands unerringly. Aiyana is willing to use the
necrophidius to help recover her estate, but
she won't needlessly sacrifice it—it's a rather
expensive construct and has been in her
family for years.

NECROPHIDIUS	CR 3

XP 800
hp 36 (*Pathfinder RPG Bestiary 2* 196)

Next Steps
Once the PCs have cleared Aiyana's estate of Reborn
occupation forces, they have a short reprieve but are by
no means safe. The estate is a fairly secure place to rest and
recover, but it will not take long for the Reborn to learn of
Aiyana's return and retaliate, even if Callivarius doesn't
manage to escape to warn them. Aiyana assures the
party that they will be safe for at least a night and
can then leave the estate locked up and sneak out
through the postern when they make their next
move. Though the PCs can make their own
plans, Aiyana has the following suggestions:

Consult Nomianna: The PCs
might consider consulting the seer
Nomianna, a fey living in a flooded
cavern just north of Lyrudrada.
Nomianna might be able to
provide advice, and her island
might provide a safe haven for
the party, since Aiyana's estate
is unlikely to remain secure for
long. Nomianna's grotto is area **C**.

Consult Shevarimarr: The cloaker
sorcerer Shevarimarr is a notorious
information broker in Traders' Rift. If anyone
can provide inside information about the Reborn and their
doings, Shevarimarr can, as he's remarkably well informed

INTRODUCTION

CHAPTER 1:
REMNANTS OF THE DARK

CHAPTER 2:
GAME OF SHADOWS

CHAPTER 3:
FATE OF THE FORSAKEN

APPENDIX 1:
LYRUDRADA

APPENDIX 2:
BESTIARY

about goings-on throughout the city. In addition, Aiyana knows him to be an expert on matters regarding the Shadow Plane, and she suspects he could likely tell the PCs more about their shadowbound corruption. Aiyana does not entirely trust Shevarimarr, but she knows him to be no friend of the Reborn. Shevarimarr's brokerage is area **D**.

Rescue the Bleakshore Council: Aiyana is very concerned about the fate of any survivors of her estate as well as the rest of the Bleakshore Council; unfortunately, she doesn't know where they might be or even whether any of them are still alive. A PC who succeeds at a DC 30 Diplomacy check to gather information about the Bleakshore Council's whereabouts turns up only a grim name: the Sadist Spires, domain of the wicked drider Ezurkian. The Sadist Spires is area **E**.

Recover the Cradle of Night: As the Reborn already have the *Cradle of Night*, it's only a matter of time before the cult dominates Lyrudrada and expands its plans even further. A raid upon the Forsaken Fane to recover the artifact and crush the cult is probably inevitable, but Aiyana recommends first gathering intelligence and potential allies. When the PCs are ready to assault the Forsaken Fane, go to Chapter 3.

Search Teams (CR 10)

The PCs can travel safely around Lyrudrada for 24 hours after their liberation of Aiyana's estate. After this time, the Reborn organize search teams to find Aiyana and the PCs. After the first 24 hours, for each hour (or fraction thereof) that the PCs or Aiyana remain on the streets and waterways of Lyrudrada, they have a 10% chance of encountering a Reborn search team described below; every 24 hours, this chance increases by 10% per hour (to a maximum of 50%). This encounter occurs automatically if the PCs are still at Aiyana's estate, as the Reborn check there first. However, the PCs should encounter no more than three search teams on any day and no more than five search teams total. After that, the umbral dragon Thelamistos begins hunting for the PCs personally, and a search team encounter is with Thelamistos instead; before that time, however, the PCs should take the fight to the Forsaken Fane.

REBORN COMMANDO	CR 7

XP 3,200
hp 91 (see page 22)

REBORN CUTTHROATS (2)	CR 7

XP 3,200 each
hp 81 each (see page 24)

C. SEER'S GROTTO

At Aiyana's suggestion, the PCs might seek out the seer Nomianna for more information. Nomianna lives on an island in the center of an underground lake north of Mudshore (location **3** on the Lyrudrada poster map).

The residents of Lyrudrada don't venture there except for rare visits seeking Nomianna's advice or blessing. They consider Nomianna to be a powerful force of nature and her cavern to be a peaceful, sacred place. The PCs should consider acquiring a boat to reach the island—the water is still but icy, and the island is several hundred feet from the shore. A flat-bottom coracle large enough to carry the entire party can be purchased for 25 gp, rented for 3 gp per day, or even stolen. When the PCs head to Nomianna's island, read or paraphrase the following.

> The cavern beyond Lyrudrada's unkempt, bustling slums is breathtaking. Absolute silence and stillness reign under this vast stone dome. The cavern's vaulted ceiling, above a dark lake of perfectly smooth water, is alight with thousands of phosphorescent glowworms. Together, they resemble a starry sky, twinkling as the glowworms wriggle. The reflection of these twinkling lights upon the water gives the impression of floating through a sea of stars. A stone jetty extends from a small, rocky island in the lake's center.

Nomianna lives in a grotto on the island in the lake. The lake waters flow into the grotto from underwater passages (area **C3**), although the easiest entry to the grotto is the cave near the jetty. The glowworms provide the cavern with dim light, but the grotto interior is dark except in Nomianna's gallery (area **C4**).

C1. Grotto Entry (CR 9)

> This low cave leads into a grotto at the island's center. The gentle splash of water echoes throughout the cave.

Although most residents of Lyrudrada treat Nomianna with a balance of suspicion and reverence, the Reborn worry that Nomianna could interfere with their plans. Rather than attack the mysterious seer directly, the cult instead dispatched a pair of invisible stalkers to prevent anyone from seeking her guidance. Nomianna is aware of them, but hasn't yet determined what to do.

From this entry, one path leads west to a hidden pool (area **C2**), and another to a natural stone bridge (area **C3**).

Creatures: Two invisible stalkers watch over this entry. Bored at their guard duty, the creatures are eager for a fight but flee Lyrudrada entirely if reduced to fewer than 20 hit points.

INVISIBLE STALKERS (2)	CR 7

XP 3,200 each
hp 80 each (*Pathfinder RPG Bestiary* 181)

C2. Hidden Pool (CR 7)

> Water laps at the edge of a natural pool inside the island. Although the clear water is shallow at the edge, it becomes

much darker and deeper to the south. This chamber drips with moisture, and several stalagmites and stalactites adorn the floor and ceiling.

This peaceful pool is one of Nomianna's favorite places, although she isn't here now. The pool becomes so deep here that it connects to watery chambers in a lower section of the Darklands. Nomianna sometimes receives visitors from that distant region, although no one else in Lyrudrada knows about this passage to deeper lands.

To the south, cliffs lead up to area **C4**; those cliffs are only 20 feet tall but exceptionally slick, requiring a successful DC 30 Climb check to ascend.

Creatures: Three tentamorts found their way into this cavern several days ago; Nomianna isn't yet aware of their presence, as she hasn't been to the north side of the pool recently. The tentamorts cling to the ceiling over the edge of the pool until prey wanders near.

TENTAMORTS (3)	CR 4

XP 1,200 each

hp 39 each (*Pathfinder RPG Bestiary 2* 261)

C3. Natural Bridge

This graceful, natural stone bridge arches over the small stream connecting the hidden pool (area **C2**) to the larger lake surrounding the island.

C4. Nomianna's Gallery (CR 6)

This stony chamber contains several elegant ridges of stone that appear too delicate to have formed naturally, yet they remain unmarked by tools or other evidence of workmanship. To the west, the chamber drops off sharply into a pool below. Several glowworms, like those in the cavern outside, provide dim illumination throughout this chamber.

Nomianna has specifically cultivated the glowworms here in her gallery for the effect their light has upon the stone sculptures she slowly and carefully creates.

Creature: Nomianna is a lampad with lustrous ebony skin and silver hair. If Nomianna knows the PCs are present, she hides among her sculptures until she judges whether they are threats. She warns the PCs to keep their distance, as she knows the erratic effects her insane beauty aura can produce. As long as the PCs demonstrate peaceful intentions, Nomianna is willing to talk with them, although she worries about a Reborn trick.

Nomianna's starting attitude to the PCs is unfriendly, unless the PCs defeated the invisible stalkers (in which case it is indifferent). If the PCs can modify Nomianna's attitude to friendly or helpful, she allows the PCs to use her grotto as a base camp for as long as they like and uses her spells to aid them.

Nomianna

NOMIANNA	CR 6

XP 2,400

Female advanced lampad (*Pathfinder RPG Bestiary 4* 288, 178)

hp 66

D. SHEVARIMARR'S BROKERAGE

The cloaker sorcerer Shevarimarr is something of a curiosity in Lyrudrada: he runs a curio shop in the Trader's Rift district, but this shop primarily serves as an ill-disguised front for his more lucrative business as an information broker. Shevarimarr is something of an expert on all things regarding the Shadow Plane, which often surprises his caligni clients. Aiyana has never met Shevarimarr before, but she knows enough about him to recommend that the PCs seek him out. The PCs can acquire directions to his brokerage with a successful DC 10 Diplomacy check to gather information in Traders' Rift.

Shevarimarr's brokerage is a series of chambers cut into the wall of an isolated arm branching from Traders' Rift (location **4** on the Lyrudrada poster map). Its recessed door is an arching construction of ancient wood taken from some uplander sailing ship of unknown provenance, and next to it the mounted skull of a cave raptor clutches a signboard in its mouth painted with the words "Always Open" in both Dark Folk and Undercommon. The shop itself is a smoky, shadowy, claustrophobic place filled with a clutter of indescribable objects, dimly glowing incense burners, and the unpleasant odors of mildew and decomposition. The ceilings in the brokerage are only 6 feet high, but despite the brokerage's confining nature, Shevarimarr has no trouble moving about due to his flexible physiology. Shevarimarr spends most of his time meditating in his den (area **D4**), so the PCs must make their way through his shop to engage his services.

D1. Curio Displays

This chamber is cluttered with an eclectic array of strange metal devices, chipped sculptures, and general junk. An archway leads to a wide passage leading south.

This chamber is where Shevarimarr keeps his least valuable curios, as the occasional thief or ill-mannered

INTRODUCTION

CHAPTER 1:
REMNANTS OF THE DARK

CHAPTER 2:
GAME OF SHADOWS

CHAPTER 3:
FATE OF THE FORSAKEN

APPENDIX 1:
LYRUDRADA

APPENDIX 2:
BESTIARY

patron attempts to filch items from this room. He instead brings out truly valuable items for display to customers who demonstrate the ability to pay. A PC who succeeds at a DC 20 Appraise check realizes that there is very little of true interest or value to be found in this room.

The archway leads to the reading alcoves (area **D2**). The creatures there are making enough noise that a PC can overhear their scuttling with a successful DC 22 Perception check.

D2. Reading Alcoves (CR 7)

Four alcoves opening off this long hall each contain a reading table positioned in front of floor-to-ceiling curtains. The curtains aren't fully drawn, revealing shelves behind them piled with scrolls, tomes, and folios. Several crates are stacked near some of the reading tables like impromptu stools.

The reading materials in these alcoves cover a wide variety of topics, although they aren't particularly well organized. Shevarimarr allows customers to rent these alcoves and peruse his available texts at a rate of 1 sp per hour, though he doesn't allow the reading materials to be removed from the shop. As with the jumbled bric-a-brac of the curio displays (area **D1**), none of these texts are particularly valuable.

Creatures: A misdirected shipment led to a crate containing three albino cave solifugids being delivered to the brokerage (Shevarimarr believes the crate to contain secondhand books and hasn't yet dealt with it). The creatures escaped the crate only a few minutes ago and are currently chewing through the assorted scrolls here in search of food. When they detect the PCs' presence, they rush forward, seeking a quick meal. These creatures are hungry enough to fight to the death.

ALBINO CAVE SOLIFUGIDS (3)	CR 4

XP 1,200 each

hp 45 each (*Pathfinder RPG Bestiary 2* 253)

D3. Storage (CR 8)

The wooden door to this room is locked (hardness 5, hp 20, break DC 23, Disable Device 35), and Shevarimarr keeps the only key. The room is lined with shelves holding a dizzying assortment of jewelry, magic items, and works of art. This is a good place for the GM to include any specific items that would be useful to provide to the PCs, as Shevarimarr's taste is highly eclectic. Otherwise, it contains 30,000 gp of nonmagical goods and 1d4+2 items listed for sale in the Lyrudrada city stat block (see page 57).

Creature: Among the items stored in here is a simple bottle containing a polong that has been under Shevarimarr's control for many months. The polong attacks anyone entering this room that isn't accompanied by Shevarimarr. The cloaker rarely lets the spirit vent its

pent-up anger, so it relishes any opportunity to engage in combat. It fights until destroyed or until Shevarimarr orders it to return to its bottle.

POLONG	CR 8

XP 4,800

hp 95 (*Pathfinder RPG Bestiary 5* 196)

D4. Shevarimarr's Den (CR 9)

This chamber is just as cluttered as the rest of the shop, but contains no furniture. Instead, items are stacked haphazardly across the floor or in teetering piles against the walls. A few tapestries featuring abstract mixtures of texture and color adorn several of the walls near iron hooks, and two incredibly lifelike statues lean against the south wall.

This is Shevarimarr's personal quarters, and it lacks any ordinary furnishings, since due to his unusual physiology, the cloaker doesn't need them. The tapestries are considered incredibly artistic among cloakers, and the two statues—a drow priestess and a hobgoblin warlord—are actually the petrified victims of a basilisk, which Shevarimarr purchased as art objects.

Creature: When Shevarimarr isn't meeting with customers, he meditates here in his quarters, folded around one of the hooks and appearing as a hanging cloak. Sometimes, as now, Shevarimarr's meditation is deep enough that he ignores activity in the rest of his shop, although he is quick to greet anyone who enters this room. Shevarimarr is vain and has a tendency to finish his guests' sentences for them (usually in a manner entirely unlike what his visitors planned to say). Despite his frequent meditation and alien conversational habits, Shevarimarr is particularly well informed about goings-on in Lyrudrada and lore regarding the Shadow Plane.

SHEVARIMARR	CR 9

XP 6,400

Male cloaker sorcerer 7 (*Pathfinder RPG Bestiary* 47)

CN Large aberration

Init +9; **Senses** darkvision 90 ft.; Perception +16

DEFENSE

AC 23, touch 15, flat-footed 17 (+5 Dex, +1 dodge, +8 natural, −1 size)

hp 110 (13 HD; 7d6+6d8+59)

Fort +8, **Ref** +9, **Will** +13

Defensive Abilities shadow shift

OFFENSE

Speed 10 ft., fly 40 ft. (average)

Melee bite +12 (1d6+6), tail slap +7 (1d8+3)

Space 10 ft.; **Reach** 10 ft. (5 ft. with bite)

Special Attacks engulf, moan

Sorcerer Spell-Like Abilities (CL 7th; concentration +13)

9/day—shadowstrike (1d4+3 nonlethal plus dazzled)

Shevarimarr

Skills Acrobatics +5, Disguise +12 (+20 to appear as a cloak, sheet, manta ray, or similarly sized object or creature), Fly +19, Knowledge (religion) +10, Perception +16, Sense Motive +9, Stealth +17; **Racial Modifiers** +8 Disguise to appear as a cloak, sheet, manta ray, or similarly sized object or creature

Languages Dark Folk, Shadowtongue, Undercommon

SQ bloodline arcana (gain bonus on Stealth checks)

Gear *amulet of natural armor +1*, *pink and green sphere ioun stone*, key to area **D3**

Development: The PCs have likely come at Aiyana's suggestion to speak to Shevarimarr about the Reborn. Shevarimarr is indifferent toward the Reborn and would like to avoid their ire, but the shadowbound corruption the PCs bear piques his interest. The information broker offers to share what he knows with the PCs if they pay him 1,000 gp, or if they pay him 500 gp and purchase at least 5,000 gp worth of items from his shop. He doesn't negotiate the price, but his offer is genuine and, if the PCs pay it, Shevarimarr answers any questions the PCs pose about Lyrudrada, the Reborn, their shadowbound corruption, and other relevant Darklands topics to the best of his ability. This is a good opportunity for the GM to impart any information from the Adventure Background section to the PCs, as well as any or all of the following:

- General information about the shadowbound corruption as found in *Pathfinder RPG Horror Adventures*. Shevarimarr also speculates that the Forsaken Fane is likely to cause further manifestations of this corruption.

- Specific information about the *Cradle of Night* (see page 55) and how to destroy it. He theorizes that destroying it is likely the only way to remove the PCs' shadowbound corruption.

- The drider Ezurkian was involved in the raid on Aiyana's estate, and prisoners are likely still held in the drider's lair in Ragtown (location **5** on the Lyrudrada poster map). He knows that the drider keeps strange allies, but has no specific information about his home other than its location.

- "Veilisendri lifts the veil" is the passphrase that new recruits of the Reborn use to gain safe access to Ancestors' Isle (see Chapter 3). Shevarimarr isn't familiar with the layout of the Forsaken Fane on the island, but he knows it is very heavily guarded.

When the PCs' conversation with Shevarimarr is completed, consider interrupting them with the Assassins event described on page 33.

Sorcerer Spells Known (CL 7th; concentration +13)

3rd (5/day)—*deeper darkness, suggestion* (DC 19), *vampiric touch*

2nd (8/day)—*alter self, darkness, darkvision, web* (DC 18)

1st (8/day)—*charm person* (DC 17), *grease* (DC 17), *mage armor, magic missile, ray of enfeeblement* (DC 17), *unseen servant*

0 (at will)—*dancing lights, detect magic, mage hand, message, open/close* (DC 16), *prestidigitation, read magic*

Bloodline shadow[APG]

TACTICS

During Combat Shevarimarr always attempts to avoid combat, casting *deeper darkness* to cover his retreat if necessary. When combat seems unavoidable, he uses his moan and shadow shift abilities to confound his enemies and escape.

Morale Shevarimarr prefers flight to surrender, but he prefers either to being harmed.

STATISTICS

Str 23, **Dex** 20, **Con** 19, **Int** 12, **Wis** 17, **Cha** 22

Base Atk +7; **CMB** +14; **CMD** 30 (can't be tripped)

Feats Arcane Strike, Combat Casting, Combat Reflexes, Dodge, Eschew Materials, Hover, Improved Initiative, Silent Spell, Skill Focus (Perception)

Cradle of Night

INTRODUCTION

CHAPTER 1:
REMNANTS OF THE DARK

CHAPTER 2:
GAME OF SHADOWS

CHAPTER 3:
FATE OF THE FORSAKEN

APPENDIX 1:
LYRUDRADA

APPENDIX 2:
BESTIARY

The Assassins (CR 11)

The Reborn fear Shevarimarr's deep knowledge might be used against them, but they only recently became confident enough in their newfound leadership of Lyrudrada to consider eliminating him. When the Reborn saw (or suspected) that the PCs were visiting the information broker, Veilisendri resolved to kill two birds with one stone by eliminating both threats at once.

The cult's assassin team can attack any time the PCs are at the brokerage, but the attack works best if it occurs just as the PCs are wrapping up their conversation with Shevarimarr. The Reborn commandos send in their slithering trackers to lead the attack, hoping to paralyze a few of the PCs just before they burst into the room. If Shevarimarr is present when the assassins attack, he retreats to his den (area **D4**), or hides behind the tapestries hanging in his den if the attack occurs there. He doesn't emerge until the battle is over. If the PCs flee the brokerage, the assassins don't pursue, as they decide to hunt down and kill the cloaker instead.

REBORN COMMANDOS (3)	CR 7

XP 3,200 each

hp 91 each (see page 22)

ADVANCED SLITHERING TRACKERS (2)	CR 5

XP 1,600 each

hp 50 each (*Pathfinder RPG Bestiary 2* 292, 250)

Development: If the PCs defeat the assassins, rather than just fighting their way to freedom and leaving Shevarimarr to his fate, the information broker is uncharacteristically touched. He rewards them by offering the PCs use of his polong bottle (see area **D3**) when they move against the Reborn at the Forsaken Fane. He cautions them to acquire other allies and information first, if they can, but to check with him before they approach Ancestor's Isle so he can transfer control of the polong. Shevarimarr grants control of the polong (as per *dominate monster*) to a single PC for 24 hours; after that time, the polong can attempt a DC 20 Will save each day to break free from the PC's control.

E. SADIST SPIRES

The drider Ezurkian is known throughout Lyrudrada as a torturer and dabbler in enchantments. He dwells in a pair of hollow stalagmites in central Ragtown called the Sadist Spires (location **5** on the Lyrudrada poster map), the location of which can be obtained from Shevarimarr or with a successful DC 15 Diplomacy check to gather information. If the result of a PC's check to gather information about the Sadist Spires exceeds a DC of 20, the PC also learns that Ezurkian has inhabited the spires for only a few years—he tracked and murdered a renegade drow arcanist living in the spires, then simply claimed the structure as his own. If this check

result exceeds a DC of 25, the PC further learns that although the Sadist Spires has a front door, Ezurkian and his guests rarely use it, often entering the structure via one of its many balconies or the bridge connecting the two spires. All walls in the Sadist Spires are of hewn stone, and the doors are heavy fungi planks equivalent to strong wood. The ceilings are 20 feet high unless otherwise specified. All interior rooms are lit by small oil lamps set high on the wall that provide each of these areas with dim light. The exterior of the Sadist Spires is slick with condensation and requires a successful DC 25 Climb check to scale.

E1. Entrance Hall (CR 8)

The main entrance to the Sadist Spires is locked (hardness 5, hp 20, break DC 28, Disable Device DC 40), and Ezurkian has the only key to this door.

This oddly shaped chamber at the core of the stalagmite bears a pair of oil lamps in sconces hung upon buttresses in the exterior wall. The floor is covered in what must be decades of detritus composed of bits of spoiled food, the rotting carcasses of myriad animals and small creatures, and an accumulation of random debris. Patches of mushrooms and mold are scattered throughout, and the smell is atrocious.

Ezurkian uses this hall as a general dump whenever he doesn't just fling the detritus of his work off of a balcony. The floor here is difficult terrain. The doors lead outside the Sadist Spires, to the lower balcony (area **E2**), and to the stairwell (area **E3**).

Creatures: The refuse in this chamber has become the lair of six fungal crawlers that root through the garbage. Ezurkian ignores them, and they have learned to scatter and hide when the drider is present. The fungal crawlers aggressively fight other creatures that intrude into this room. When two or fewer fungal crawlers remain, they flee and try to hide.

FUNGAL CRAWLERS (6)	CR 3

XP 800 each

hp 26 each (*Pathfinder RPG Bestiary 2* 127)

E2. Lower Balcony

A low balcony with a four-foot-high stone parapet protrudes from the lower portion of this spire, twenty feet above the cavern floor. A suspension bridge stretching between the two stalagmites hangs far above.

Ezurkian rarely uses this balcony, and it bears heaps of trash like the adjacent entrance hall (area **E1**). The door between this balcony and the entrance hall once had a lock, but the mechanism long ago rusted and the door opens with a successful DC 10 Strength check.

Development: Anyone lingering openly on this balcony for more than 3 rounds draws the attentions of the skavelings circling high above the Sadist Spires; 1d3 skavelings from area **E5**, if present, swoop down to investigate the possibility of an easy meal.

E3. Stairwell (CR 6)

This stairwell is covered with broken flasks, rotting meat, and discarded rubbish, though a path has been cleared down the center of the stairway.

Like area **E1**, this stairwell has been used as a trash receptacle by Ezurkian for years. Though he cleared away the stairs a few weeks ago for a guest, he merely pushed the trash aside rather than actually removing it.

Hazard: The close confines of this stairwell make the smell of rot overpowering. Each creature in the stairwell must succeed at a DC 15 Fortitude save each round or become nauseated for 1 round; on a successful save, the creature is merely sickened for 1 round instead. This is a poison effect, and a creature can hold its breath to avoid this effect.

Creatures: Three fungal crawlers lurk here. Like those in area **E1**, they hide if Ezurkian is present. They are tenacious at defending their larder and fight until slain.

FUNGAL CRAWLERS (3)	CR 3

XP 800 each
hp 26 each (*Pathfinder RPG Bestiary 2* 127)

Development: Noisy combat here alerts Gallach in the library above (area **E4**) to trouble, and he prepares as described there.

E4. Library (CR 9)

A pair of stairways and an external door access this round, high-ceilinged chamber. One stretch of the wall is almost entirely covered in a bookcase carved from the stone wall and crammed with all manner of scrolls and tomes. Small oil lamps in high sconces provide dim illumination over a large reading table and a desk tucked into an alcove.

When Ezurkian claimed the Sadist Spires, he inherited the previous owner's extensive library of books, scrolls, and other manuscripts detailing drow life, religion, and hierarchy. There are also a number of ethnographies and histories of Darklands creatures and societies, including caligni. Anyone fluent in both Elven and Undercommon making use of this library to research a topic pertaining to Darklands matters gains a +2 circumstance bonus on the pertinent Knowledge check for each full day spent perusing this library (to a maximum bonus of +6) and can attempt such checks untrained.

Creature: A dark slayer alchemist named Gallach accompanied the owb sorcerer Xhamila (see area **E7**) on a visit to Ezurkian. Although Ezurkian is polite—even servile—to Xhamila, the drider is less pleasant to Gallach, and the caligni stays out of the way here. Scrawny and bookish, Gallach has had to rely on his intellect rather than his physique for most of his life, and he's used to solving problems with calculated precision. Gallach hopes to find new formulae or at least information that might be useful to the Reborn to improve his standing within the group. He is not expecting an attack and is prepared for combat only if alerted by the sounds of combat from areas **E3** or **E7**.

GALLACH	CR 9

XP 6,400
Male dark slayer alchemist 8 (*Pathfinder RPG Bestiary 2* 75, *Pathfinder RPG Advanced Player's Guide* 26)
CE Small humanoid (dark folk)
Init +5; **Senses** *detect magic*, see in darkness; Perception +20

DEFENSE

AC 24, touch 17, flat-footed 18 (+4 armor, +5 Dex, +1 dodge, +3 natural, +1 size)
hp 110 (12d8+56)
Fort +10, **Ref** +15, **Will** +6; +6 vs. poison
Weaknesses light blindness

OFFENSE

Speed 30 ft.
Melee mwk kukri +16/+11 (1d3–2/18–20)
Ranged bomb +16/+11 touch (4d6+3 fire) or
   force bomb +16/+11 touch (4d4+3 force) or
   frost bomb +16/+11 touch (4d6+3 cold)
Special Attacks bomb 11/day (4d6+3 fire, DC 17), death throes, sneak attack +2d6
Spell-Like Abilities (CL 4th; concentration +6)
   Constant—*detect magic*
   At will—*bleed* (DC 12), *chill touch* (DC 13), *darkness*,
      spectral hand
   3/day—*daze monster* (DC 14), *death knell* (DC 14), *inflict
      moderate wounds* (DC 14)
Alchemist Extracts Prepared (CL 8th; concentration +11)
   3rd—*displacement, fly, protection from energy*
   2nd—*barkskin, cure moderate wounds, invisibility, shadow
      bomb admixture*^UC, *touch injection*^UC
   1st—*bomber's eye*^APG, *cure light wounds, disguise self,
      shield, true strike*

TACTICS

Before Combat If warned that combat might be imminent, Gallach prepares by using his *wand of mirror image* and consuming his *barkskin* and *displacement* extracts. If the opportunity presents itself before hostilities begin, Gallach uses his *wand of charm monster* on the toughest opponent.
During Combat Gallach tries to keep his distance and throw bombs; as the library isn't his, he doesn't exercise any restraint when it comes to hurling bombs around the room.

INTRODUCTION

CHAPTER 1:
REMNANTS OF THE DARK

CHAPTER 2:
GAME OF SHADOWS

CHAPTER 3:
FATE OF THE FORSAKEN

APPENDIX 1:
LYRUDRADA

APPENDIX 2:
BESTIARY

Morale If reduced to fewer than 40 hit points, Gallach makes a fighting retreat to Xhamila's side (area **E7**). There, he surrenders or flees only if Xhamila is defeated or escapes.

Base Statistics Without *barkskin*, Gallach's statistics are AC 21, touch 17, flat-footed 15.

STATISTICS

Str 7, **Dex** 20, **Con** 16, **Int** 16, **Wis** 13, **Cha** 15

Base Atk +9; **CMB** +6; **CMD** 22

Feats Brew Potion, Dodge, Iron Will, Point-Blank Shot, Skill Focus (Use Magic Device), Throw Anything, Toughness, Weapon Finesse

Skills Climb +2, Craft (alchemy) +18 (+26 to create alchemical items), Fly +16, Knowledge (arcana, local, nature, planes) +7, Perception +20, Sleight of Hand +20, Spellcraft +18, Stealth +13, Use Magic Device +23; **Racial Modifiers** +4 Climb, +4 Perception, +4 Stealth

Languages Aklo, Dark Folk, Shadowtongue, Undercommon

SQ alchemy (alchemy crafting +8), discoveries (fast bombs, force bomb, frost bomb, precise bombs [3 squares]), magical knack, mutagen (+4/−2, +2 natural armor, 80 minutes), poison use, soul harvest, swift alchemy

Combat Gear *wand of charm monster* (11 charges), *wand of lightning bolt* (15 charges), *wand of mirror image* (14 charges); **Other Gear** *+1 studded leather*, mwk kukri, alchemy crafting kit^UE, formula book (contains all prepared extracts plus 2d4 additional extracts), 37 pp, 2 gp

Treasure: Most of the texts in here are of no particular resale value, despite their use as reference materials. However, they include a *scroll of protection from chaos*, a *scroll of vermin shape II*^UM, a *scroll of serenity*^UM, a *scroll of teleport*, and a *bookmark of deception*^UE hidden inside a mundane dictionary to make it resemble a different mundane dictionary.

E5. Central Bridge (CR 9)

A suspension bridge composed of thick fungus planks held together by ropes of strong fungus fiber spans the gap between two stalagmites. The cavern floor eighty feet below is studded with sharp stalagmites.

This bridge is sturdy and in good repair, as Ezurkian uses it frequently. A rope railing on either side prevents anyone from easily falling off, but anyone jumping or falling from the bridge takes damage from the stalagmites below as if they had fallen on pit spikes. The doors at either end of the bridge lead to the library (area **E4**) and the prison (area **E6**). Both doors are unlocked.

Creatures: Four skavelings roost above the Sadist Spires and keep an eye out for promising meals. The skavelings don't attack Ezurkian or anyone they've seen accompanying the drider,

but they swoop down to attack other creatures. One of the skavelings screeches as the rest attack. The skavelings fight until destroyed.

SKAVELINGS (4)	CR 5

XP 1,600 each

hp 58 each (*Pathfinder RPG Bestiary 2* 42)

Development: If the PCs earned Shevarimarr's goodwill by defeating the assassins sent to kill him, the cloaker provides an additional token of thanks that the PCs might not even notice: he's arranged for some caligni spider-riders to scale the cavern above the Sadist Spires and chase off the skavelings roosting there. The skavelings

Gallach

therefore aren't present when the PCs first come to the Sadist Spires, but if the PCs retreat and re-enter the Sadist Spires later, the skavelings have returned.

E6. Prison (CR 6)

Much of this chamber is a large cell built out of the rock of the stalagmite itself, with two small doors made of heavy iron bars. Several iron cages, none larger than five feet square, hang from chains bolted to the ceiling or are stacked together on the floor. Bladed chains, manacles, and coils of rope hang from hooks on the wall and in piles on the floor. A key hangs from one of the hooks next to the door.

Ezurkian keeps his prisoners here until he is ready to work on them in his laboratory or between gruesome interrogation sessions. The key hanging on the wall opens the cell and cages. The main cell holds three caligni rogues, a dark stalker, and a dark creeper. All are members of the Bleakshore Council, captured by the Reborn and tortured by Ezurkian for information. Each currently has only 1d4 hit points remaining. One of the hanging cages contains a dark creeper named Bezlek. Bezlek works for the Bleakshore Council as a spy and was attempting to rescue the other captured council members when he was caught; although he hasn't yet been tortured and has all of his hit points, Ezurkian has described the painful alchemical mutations he has in mind for the spy. All of the prisoners are demoralized and fear for their lives. They can describe Ezurkian and the lower areas of the spire (areas **E8** through **E10**), as the drider takes them to his laboratory for their tortures. Bezlek also knows that Ezurkian's liaison with the Reborn is a female owb named Xhamila. These prisoners want nothing more than their freedom, so they can return to stirring up popular sentiment against the Reborn.

Creature: Unbeknownst to any of the prisoners, one of the coils of rope lying on the floor is actually a rope dragon watching the prisoners for Ezurkian. As it is currently in its discorporating coils form, the PCs must succeed at a Perception check opposed by the rope dragon's Stealth check (it has a +20 bonus) to recognize it as anything other than an old, frayed rope. If the PCs start to free the prisoners, the rope dragon reverts to its dragon form and uses its breath weapon on the PCs and as many prisoners as possible, hoping to kill them. It then flees to area **E10** to warn Ezurkian.

ADVANCED ROPE DRAGON	CR 6

XP 2,400
hp 69 (*Pathfinder RPG Bestiary 5* 288, 211)

Treasure: The rope dragon's hoard is hidden beneath a pile of rusty chains; a successful DC 21 Perception check is required to locate it. The small hoard consists of a pouch containing 84 gp, three alabaster buttons worth 35 gp each, a *scroll of detect good*, and a *bead of force*.

Story Award: Award the PCs 800 XP for each prisoner that makes it out of the Sadist Spires alive.

E7. Guest Room (CR 10)

A wide, canopied bed rests against the curve of wall that holds the stairs leading to this finely appointed chamber. Stone tables bearing crystal decanters and multicolored glass carafes stand against the sections of wall between three doorways that open out onto balconies.

Ezurkian maintains this chamber as a guest room for visiting clients. The doorways open out onto balconies with low, stone rails that provide a panoramic view of much of Ragtown and the adjacent lake. The cavern floor is 140 feet below the eastern balcony, but only 120 feet from the other two balconies, as they extend over a higher section of the cavern floor. The bridge (area **E5**) and lower balcony (area **E2**) are also visible from these balconies, although the east balcony (area **E9**) is not.

Creature: A cold, aloof owb oracle named Xhamila currently resides in this room. A liaison of the Reborn sent to obtain information about the Bleakshore Council prisoners, Xhamila is happy to let Ezurkian perform the messy business of interrogation. Xhamila arrived here with the dark slayer Gallach, whom she considers too academic to be of much use; she's happy to let Gallach spend his time in the library (area **E4**). If she encounters the PCs, Xhamila considers it her primary duty to see how they fight firsthand and report back to Veilisendri. The PCs might face her again in the Forsaken Fane (see area **F10**).

XHAMILA	CR 10

XP 9,600
Female owb oracle 7 (*Pathfinder RPG Bestiary 4* 210, *Pathfinder RPG Advanced Player's Guide* 42)
NE Medium outsider (extraplanar)
Init +11; **Senses** darkvision 60 ft., see in darkness; Perception +17

DEFENSE

AC 26, touch 20, flat-footed 16 (+6 armor, +2 deflection, +7 Dex, +1 dodge)
hp 127 (15 HD; 7d8+8d10+52); fast healing 2
Fort +13, **Ref** +13, **Will** +16; +2 vs. death effects, disease, mind-affecting effects, poison, sleep, and stunning
Immune cold
Weaknesses light sensitivity

OFFENSE

Speed 5 ft., fly 60 ft. (perfect)
Melee 2 claws +19 (1d8+6 plus 1d6 cold)
Ranged burning cold +20 touch (3d6 cold)
Special Attacks burning cold, curse of darkness

Xhamila

Spell-Like Abilities (CL 8th; concentration +14)

Constant—*blur*

At will—*deeper darkness, detect thoughts* (DC 18), *dust of twilight*^{APG} (DC 18)

5/day—*shadow step*^{UM}

1/day—*plane shift* (self only, to or from Shadow Plane only)

Oracle Spells Known (CL 7th; concentration +13)

3rd (5/day)—*animate dead, bestow curse* (DC 19), *dispel magic, inflict serious wounds* (DC 19)

2nd (8/day)—*false life, hold person* (DC 18), *inflict moderate wounds* (DC 18), *lesser restoration, levitate, minor image* (DC 18), *sound burst* (DC 18)

1st (8/day)—*cause fear* (DC 17), *command* (DC 17), *doom* (DC 17), *inflict light wounds* (DC 17), *ray of sickening*^{UM} (DC 17), *sanctuary* (DC 17), *shield of faith*

0 (at will)—*bleed* (DC 16), *detect magic, ghost sound* (DC 16), *guidance, mage hand, mending, read magic, resistance, stabilize*

Mystery bones

TACTICS

Before Combat Xhamila keeps her armor of bones active, as she doesn't fully trust Ezurkian. She casts *deeper darkness* and *invisibility* if given time before battle.

During Combat Xhamila attempts to hover out of melee to cast *ray of sickening* and use her burning cold ability. In melee, she casts *bestow curse* and her *inflict* spells.

Morale After 3 rounds of combat, or if reduced to fewer than 80 hit points, Xhamila flees to the Forsaken Fane.

STATISTICS

Str 22, **Dex** 24, **Con** 17, **Int** 11, **Wis** 17, **Cha** 22

Base Atk +13; **CMB** +19; **CMD** 39

Feats Combat Casting, Combat Reflexes, Dodge, Eschew Materials, Flyby Attack, Improved Initiative, Mobility, Point-Blank Shot

Skills Bluff +15, Diplomacy +14, Fly +19, Knowledge (planes) +11, Knowledge (religion) +18, Linguistics +3, Perception +17, Sense Motive +14, Spellcraft +7, Stealth +25

Languages Aklo, Common, Dark Folk, Shadowtongue (can't speak); telepathy 100 ft.

SQ oracle's curse (haunted), revelations (armor of bones, near death, soul siphon)

Gear *cloak of resistance +2, headband of alluring charisma +2, ring of protection +2*

Development: The skavelings that lurk above the Sadist Spires won't attack anyone on the balconies of this room, as Ezurkian has arranged for his guests' safety. However, PCs looking out over Ragtown might spot the umbral dragon Thelamistos (see area **F9**) checking in on Xhamila and keeping an eye out for the PCs. The dragon is coiled around a stalactite a few hundred yards away from the top of the Sadist Spires. Although Thelamistos has a good view of anyone stepping out onto the balconies around this room, PCs must succeed at a DC 25 Perception check to spot the dragon. If noticed, Thelamistos doesn't fight, but retreats to the Forsaken Fane.

E8. Drider's Den (CR 6)

Two doorways open out of this large circular chamber to the east, and a stairwell curves up along its west side. The entire room is shrouded in deep shadows and dust-covered cobwebs. A large knot of thick webbing forms a nest, and next to this nest

INTRODUCTION

CHAPTER 1:
REMNANTS OF THE DARK

CHAPTER 2:
GAME OF SHADOWS

CHAPTER 3:
FATE OF THE FORSAKEN

APPENDIX 1:
LYRUDRADA

APPENDIX 2:
BESTIARY

hangs a cocooned humanoid figure. Only the man's face and hands protrude from the webs. It appears to have once been a drow, but now its ebony skin is shrunken tight and faded to a dusky gray, and its jaw hangs open. Near the center of the chamber is a wide well from which an acrid miasma issues.

This chamber is Ezurkian's den. It was once the bedchamber of the drow arcanist Selmuirgist, whose dried and shriveled corpse still hangs near the drider's nest as a grisly trophy of his victory. The well has rough-hewn sides (Climb DC 20) and descends 40 feet through darkness into area **E10**. A thick curtain of webbing across the bottom of the well blocks light and muffles noise (imposing a –10 penalty on Perception checks), but the webbing isn't thick enough to impede movement or arrest a fall.

Trap: Ezurkian hides his treasure in an old wine cask at the back of his nest. The wine cask is trapped to spray a slurry of foul-smelling digestive enzymes that produce blinding fumes.

ACID SLURRY TRAP	CR 6

XP 2,400

Type mechanical; **Perception** DC 25; **Disable Device** DC 18

EFFECTS

Trigger touch; **Reset** none; **Bypass** hidden switch (Perception DC 30)

Effect acidic slurry (6d6 acid and permanent blindness, Fortitude DC 17 halves damage and negates blindness); multiple targets (all targets in a 10-ft. line)

Treasure: Ezurkian's treasure is hidden in a compartment in the trapped cask. It consists of 232 gp, 78 pp, two *potions of cure serious wounds*, and a *pearl of power* (1st).

E9. East Balcony (CR 8)

This low balcony looks out over the slums of Ragtown. A constant drip from the cavern ceiling high above has created an immense, foul-smelling puddle across the southern half of the balcony, and a riotous profusion of mold and fungus grows within the oily pool.

This balcony is 30 feet above the cavern floor, and the moisture makes climbing up to this balcony slightly more difficult than elsewhere in the Sadist Spires (Climb DC 30).

Creatures: Ezurkian never comes out to this balcony because the constant moisture has allowed an infestation of phycomids to sprout. The phycomids are content to remain here, feeding on the mineral-rich moisture and any creatures that come within reach of their acidic pellets. Although the skavelings roosting above the Sadist Spires are supposed to keep watch on this balcony as well, they've learned to avoid it due to the aggressive phycomids.

PHYCOMIDS (4)	CR 4

XP 1,200 each

hp 39 each (*Pathfinder RPG Bestiary 2* 210)

Treasure: A PC who succeeds at a DC 28 Perception check locates a *wand of ash storm*[UM] dropped here long ago and forgotten amid the fungal profusion.

E10. Laboratory (CR 11)

Several standing lamps impart a smoky, dim glow to this underground chamber. Two large cages of iron bars have been built into the north and east walls, both equipped with manacles and the bony remnants of past occupants. The western wall is piled with boxes and barrels of assorted components, reagents, and equipment, while the south wall has a stone table fitted with manacles and the pale form of a writhing prisoner.

Ezurkian uses this room as a laboratory and torture chamber, plying prisoners with physical, magical, and alchemical tortures that weaken the mind and loosen the tongue. The room's only exit is a hole in the ceiling, 20 feet above the floor, leading up to the well in area **E8**.

Aiyana's chamberlain **Grutise** (LN male caligni expert 5) is currently strapped to the torture table. Grutise was brought here for questioning along with the rest of the captives from Bleakshore. He's already told Ezurkian all he knows, but Ezurkian doesn't intend to let him go.

Creatures: The drider Ezurkian is present in this chamber. If the rope dragon from area **E6** warned Ezurkian, then the dragon is curled up among the assorted equipment and Ezurkian is clinging to the ceiling in the northeast corner of the room, invisible, to ambush the PCs. If not, Ezurkian is alone as he fusses over Grutise. Whether or not he is prepared to ambush the PCs, Ezurkian's first action is to use a quickened *mage hand* to tip a precariously balanced clay pot that shatters on the floor and releases a pair of heaving lumps of flesh: undigested swarms created by the drider's alchemy. The undigested swarms are indiscriminate in their attacks and fight until destroyed.

EZURKIAN	CR 10

XP 9,600

Male drider enchanter 3 (*Pathfinder RPG Bestiary* 113)

CE Large aberration

Init +4; **Senses** darkvision 120 ft., *detect good, detect law, detect magic*; Perception +19

DEFENSE

AC 25, touch 13, flat-footed 21 (+4 armor, +3 Dex, +1 dodge, +8 natural, –1 size)

hp 125 (12 HD; 3d6+9d8+75)

Fort +10, **Ref** +7, **Will** +13

Immune sleep; **SR** 18

OFFENSE

Speed 30 ft., climb 20 ft.

Cradle of Night

INTRODUCTION

CHAPTER 1:
REMNANTS OF THE DARK

CHAPTER 2:
GAME OF SHADOWS

CHAPTER 3:
FATE OF THE FORSAKEN

APPENDIX 1:
LYRUDRADA

APPENDIX 2:
BESTIARY

Melee *rod of withering* +8/+3 touch (1d4 Str and 1d4 Con), bite +4 (1d4+1 plus poison)

Space 10 ft.; **Reach** 5 ft.

Special Attacks web (+9 ranged, DC 20, 12 hp)

Spell-Like Abilities (CL 9th; concentration +11)

Constant—*detect good, detect law, detect magic*

At will—*dancing lights, darkness, faerie fire*

1/day—*clairaudience/clairvoyance, deeper darkness, dispel magic, levitate, suggestion* (DC 17)

Enchanter Spell-Like Abilities (CL 3rd; concentration +5)

8/day—*dazing touch*

Enchanter Spells Prepared (CL 9th; concentration +14)

5th—*dominate person* (DC 21), *hold monster* (DC 21), *wall of force*

4th—*charm monster* (DC 20), *confusion* (DC 20), *dimension door*, quickened *mage hand*

3rd—*fly, hold person* (DC 19), *lightning bolt* (3, DC 18)

2nd—*glitterdust* (DC 17), *hideous laughter* (DC 18), *invisibility, mirror image, scorching ray* (2)

1st—*charm person* (DC 17), *mage armor* (3), *magic missile* (2)

0 (at will)—*acid splash, ghost sound* (DC 15), *mage hand, prestidigitation*

Opposition Schools divination, necromancy

TACTICS

Before Combat Ezurkian has *mage armor* active at all times. If he suspects intruders, he also casts *invisibility* and *fly*.

During Combat After releasing the undigested swarms with a quickened *mage hand*, Ezurkian affects as many foes as possible with *confusion* before resorting to single-target spells such as *dominate person* and *hold monster*. If his foes are resistant to his enchantments, he relies on his evocation spells and attacks with his *rod of withering*.

Morale If reduced below 25 hit points, Ezurkian casts *dimension door* to reach area **E8** and then seals off the well with a *wall of force*. He drinks the potions in the cache in his nest (if they are still there) before dismissing the *wall of force* and picking off PCs who try to climb out of the well.

Base Statistics Without *mage armor*, Ezurkian's statistics are **AC** 21, touch 13, flat-footed 17.

STATISTICS

Str 15, **Dex** 17, **Con** 22, **Int** 20, **Wis** 18, **Cha** 14

Base Atk +7; **CMB** +10; **CMD** 24 (36 vs. trip)

Feats Combat Casting, Craft Rod, Dodge, Quicken Spell, Scribe Scroll, Spell Focus (enchantment), Weapon Finesse

Skills Bluff +4, Climb +22, Craft (alchemy) +14, Diplomacy +16, Fly +10, Intimidate +19, Knowledge (arcana) +20, Perception +19, Sense Motive +16, Spellcraft +17, Stealth +18; **Racial Modifiers** +4 Stealth

Languages Aklo, Common, Dark Folk, Elven, Undercommon

SQ arcane bond (*rod of withering*), enchanting smile (+2), undersized weapons

Gear *rod of withering*, spell component pouch, spellbook (contains all prepared spells plus 2d6 additional spells)

UNDIGESTED SWARMS (2)   **CR 5**

XP 1,600 each

hp 54 each (*Pathfinder RPG Bestiary 5* 258)

Treasure: This room contains an alchemical lab and assorted alchemical reagents that are worth a total of 2,000 gp but weigh 250 pounds altogether.

Story Award: Award the PCs 1,200 XP if Grutise makes it out of the Sadist Spires alive.

Ezurkian

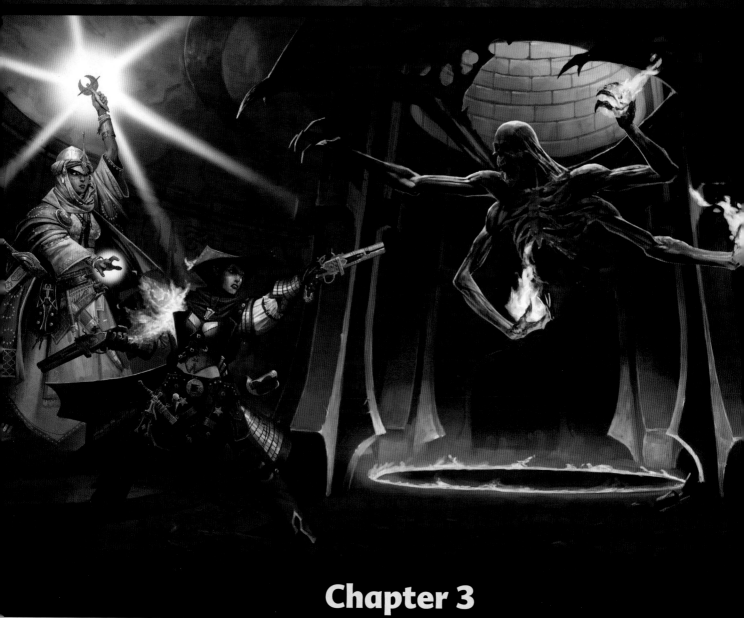

Chapter 3
Fate of the Forsaken

The Forsaken Fane, the ancient temple serving as the Reborn's headquarters, lies on Ancestors' Isle in the city's central lake (location **6** on the Lyrudrada poster map). Water traffic is not uncommon in Lyrudrada, so the PCs can easily procure a boat to reach the island, just as they did to reach Nomianna's island in Chapter 2. The greater difficulty is that a disorganized shantytown populated entirely by Reborn converts has sprung up across the lower reaches of Ancestors' Isle. More than 100 caligni of various types now dwell on the island's shores. Everyone on this island knows the passphrase taught to new recruits: "Veilisendri lifts the veil." The PCs can learn this passphrase from Shevarimarr (see area **D4**) or by succeeding at a DC 25 Diplomacy check to gather information about the Reborn anywhere in Lyrudrada.

Ancestors' Isle Patrol (CR 10)

Creatures: A vigilant patrol consisting of a Reborn officer and two Reborn commandos intercepts the PCs arriving at the docks, or at the shore within sight of the docks. As long as the new arrivals give the passphrase, they are ushered into the shantytown unimpeded (but warned not to approach the Forsaken Fane without prior approval, as the holy site is diligently guarded). If the PCs fail to provide the correct passphrase, the Reborn immediately attack, determined to repel the intruders. These cultists are so sure in their faith that they fight to the death.

PCs who don't have (or don't wish to use) the passphrase might find other ways to sneak through the shantytown or access the Forsaken Fane undetected; the success of these endeavors is subject to your discretion.

INTRODUCTION

CHAPTER 1:
REMNANTS OF THE DARK

CHAPTER 2:
GAME OF SHADOWS

CHAPTER 3:
FATE OF THE FORSAKEN

APPENDIX 1:
LYRUDRADA

APPENDIX 2:
BESTIARY

REBORN OFFICER	CR 7

XP 3,200

hp 85 (see page 22)

REBORN COMMANDOS (2)	CR 7

XP 3,200 each

hp 91 each (see page 22)

F. FORSAKEN FANE

The Forsaken Fane dates back to the early days of the Age of Darkness when the enigmatic Forsaken first reached out to the survivors of Calignos. The fane is carved out of the massive stone column that rises from Ancestors' Isle to the cavern's ceiling hundreds of feet above, though towers and a curtain wall have been constructed of masonry to supplement its defenses. The main structure has withstood the test of time and is surprisingly intact considering its age and the fact that Haramil and his forces invaded it long ago. Its interior doors are composed of 2-inch-thick stone carefully mounted on pivots. The doors can be locked by engaging bolts that slide into the floor at the base of the door; they do not use keys. The temple has very few furnishings or other ornaments, as these were all destroyed or looted by Haramil.

The fane's outer walls and towers have not fared as well with the passage of time, and many sections show signs of recent, hasty repair. The curtain wall is 40 feet high, and its towers are 60 feet tall. The towers are solid stone except for a single floor 40 feet above the ground, accessible by walkways atop the curtain wall. Climbing the crumbled stone requires a successful DC 25 Climb check.

Several areas of the fane have sheets of strange, shadowy webs clinging to the ceilings, floors, and walls. These are generally at the periphery of the rooms and hallways, leaving most of the floor space clear unless otherwise indicated. These are penumbral webs created by the nimbral child in area **F24**; see page 61 for details of the effects of these penumbral webs. Because these penumbral webs all come from this nimbral child, when the creature is destroyed, all the penumbral webs throughout the fane disintegrate in 1d4 rounds.

The ceilings are 40 feet high unless otherwise noted. The entire fane is cold, dark, and prone to echoes except in areas with penumbral webs, which feel muffled and claustrophobic. The temple's atmosphere is heavy with the weight of immense age and the almost palpable darkness that inhabits it.

F1. Outer Courtyard (CR 7)

Between the gate's towers, each looming sixty feet tall, a wide courtyard leads to a set of gates in the central pillar of the island. The courtyard is long untended and overgrown with thorny subterranean vines. A meandering path leads through the vines.

The Spreading Stain

As the PCs venture onto Ancestors' Isle in this chapter, they are exposed to greater manifestations of their shadowbound corruption. Each time the party enters one of the areas listed below, they are exposed to a greater manifestation of their corruption. They become aware of this exposure right away and can accept it and immediately gain the requisite manifestation level and its associated gift and stain, or they can attempt to resist these effects. PCs who resist can attempt a Will save (DC = 15 + current manifestation level) to avoid gaining the manifestation level. However, as long as they remain exposed to the conditions that provoke the acquisition of the new manifestation level, they must attempt a new saving throw every minute, with a cumulative –1 penalty for each minute of exposure. Becoming exposed to a later trigger before acquiring an earlier manifestation might cause a PC to gain multiple manifestations at once to "catch up," with a separate saving throw to resist each, if the PC chooses.

Corruption Trigger	Manifestation Level (and Manifestation)
Stepping foot on Ancestors' Isle	2nd (wretched pain)
Making physical contact with penumbral webs (areas **F10**, **F11**, **F20**, **F22**, **F23**, **F24**, and **F25**)	3rd (insubstantiality)
Encountering a bodak (areas **F20** and **F23**), nimbral child (area **F24**), Nhamino (area **F25**), or Veilisendri (area **F26**)	4th (refuge in pain)

The mighty gate that once blocked the courtyard was shattered in Haramil's attack long ago and has not been replaced. Ordinarily, a pair of dark champions waits here to take the passphrase and escort visitors to the temple entrance (area **F6**) along the meandering—but safe—path through the courtyard. However, because the Reborn are on high alert due to the PCs' actions, the PCs must reach the temple entrance on their own through what has become a kill zone, making it past the guards waiting in the towers (areas **F2** to **F5**), the cave giants on the defensive balconies (areas **F7a** and **F7b**), and the dark champions and their ally watching from the temple entrance.

The winding path is 160 feet long and switches back and forth through the nettle-filled courtyard in a very indirect route. Traveling across the nettles is fairly straightforward but alerts the creatures inhabiting them.

Creatures: The vines mask the presence of six mire nettles that have grown up in the courtyard. They don't bother anyone walking on the convoluted path through the courtyard, but they attack anyone who steps off the path. They fight to the death.

MIRE NETTLES (6)	CR 2

XP 600 each

hp 22 each (*Pathfinder RPG Bestiary 6* 188)

Development: The guards in the towers and on the defensive balconies have been warned of the PCs and are not likely to be caught unaware. Unless the PCs are particularly stealthy, they are likely to be subject to an overwhelming amount of ballista fire and may need to retreat to recover or develop an alternate plan of attack.

F2. Eastern Watchtower (CR 9)

This massive double tower has multiple openings 40 feet above the ground, each with ballistae on hinged swivels to allow a wide field of fire, including almost straight downward to the ground below. The openings have a low parapet wall, granting cover to anyone in the towers from attacks originating outside of them.

Although this tower used to access the Forsaken Fane, an ancient earthquake sealed off the curtain wall from the fane's interior. Now it's accessible only by ladders made of fungal fibers that can be lowered from the firing parapets.

Creatures: A dark champion leads eight dark creepers in the defense of these towers. Against intruders approaching the fane or in the courtyard below, the dark creepers operate the ballistae (*Pathfinder RPG Core Rulebook* 435) in teams of two. If intruders enter this tower, the dark champion leads the attack while the dark creepers attempt to flank the PCs. The dark champion fights until slain, but a dark creeper who is injured attempts to flee if the dark champion has already been defeated.

DARK CHAMPION	CR 5

XP 1,600

hp 59 (see page 60)

DARK CREEPERS (8)	CR 2

XP 600 each

hp 19 each (*Pathfinder RPG Bestiary* 53)

F3. Western Watchtower (CR 9)

This tower loosely resembles the eastern watchtowers (area **F2**), although it provides access to both area **F4** and the curtain wall, therefore lacking the fungal-rope ladders.

Creatures: This tower is defended by a dark champion and eight dark creepers, who fight in the same manner as the team in area **F2**.

DARK CHAMPION	CR 5

XP 1,600

hp 59 (see page 60)

DARK CREEPERS (8)	CR 2

XP 600 each

hp 19 each (*Pathfinder RPG Bestiary* 53)

Development: If a fight breaks out in this room, Kestavi comes from area **F4** to investigate immediately. So long as Kestavi remains in the fight, the dark creepers are too terrified of her to flee.

F4. Yard Commander's Post (CR 10)

This tower room has been given over to serve as personal quarters for the yard commander, a conjurer named Kestavi. The chamber has two ballistae, although they aren't normally deployed, as Kestavi doesn't use them and doesn't let the dark creepers who do into her chamber.

Creature: The gaunt and unpleasant dark slayer Kestavi is usually found here studying her spellbook. Kestavi responds to intruders in areas **F1** through **F6**, using her dimensional steps ability to gain an advantageous position, although she's been ordered not to leave the wall in case an attack is a distraction for a larger invasion.

KESTAVI	CR 10

XP 9,600

Female dark slayer conjurer 9 (*Pathfinder RPG Bestiary 2* 75)

CE Small humanoid (dark folk)

Init +6; **Senses** detect magic, see in darkness; Perception +18

DEFENSE

AC 24, touch 18, flat-footed 17 (+4 armor, +6 Dex, +1 dodge, +2 natural, +1 size)

hp 123 (13 HD; 9d6+4d8+74)

Fort +8, **Ref** +13, **Will** +8

Weaknesses light blindness

OFFENSE

Speed 30 ft.

Melee mwk kukri +15/+10 (1d3–1/18–20 plus poison)

Special Attacks death throes, sneak attack +2d6

Spell-Like Abilities (CL 4th; concentration +5)

Constant—*detect magic*

At will—*bleed* (DC 11), *chill touch* (DC 12), *darkness*, *spectral hand*

3/day—*daze monster* (DC 13), *death knell* (DC 13), *inflict moderate wounds* (DC 13)

Conjurer Spell-Like Abilities (CL 9th; concentration +14)

At will—*dimensional steps* (270 feet/day)

8/day—*acid dart* (1d6+4 acid)

Conjurer Spells Prepared (CL 9th; concentration +14)

5th—*feeblemind* (DC 20), *shadow evocation* (DC 20), *summon monster V*

4th—*acid pit*^APG (DC 20), *confusion* (DC 19), *enervation*, *summon monster IV*

3rd—*dispel magic*, *displacement*, *summon monster III*, *vampiric touch* (2)

2nd—*acid arrow*, *create pit*^APG (DC 18), *ghoul touch* (DC 17), *glitterdust* (2, DC 18), *web* (DC 18)

Cradle of Night

INTRODUCTION

CHAPTER 1:
REMNANTS OF THE DARK

CHAPTER 2:
GAME OF SHADOWS

CHAPTER 3:
FATE OF THE FORSAKEN

APPENDIX 1:
LYRUDRADA

APPENDIX 2:
BESTIARY

1st—*charm person* (DC 16), *grease* (2), *mage armor* (2), *ray of enfeeblement* (DC 16), *shield*

0 (at will)—*acid splash*, *ghost sound* (DC 15), *read magic*, *touch of fatigue* (DC 15)

Opposition Schools evocation, transmutation

TACTICS

Before Combat Kestavi casts *mage armor* early each day. Before battle, she drinks her *potion of bear's endurance*.

During Combat Kestavi casts *summon monster* spells from a distance to support her troops' attacks. She targets spellcasters with *feeblemind* and *enervation*.

Morale Kestavi is fanatically loyal to the Reborn and defends her post to the death.

Base Statistics Without *bear's endurance* and *mage armor*, Kestavi's statistics are **AC** 20, touch 18, flat-footed 13; **hp** 97; **Fort** +6; **Con** 14.

STATISTICS

Str 9, **Dex** 22, **Con** 18, **Int** 20, **Wis** 13, **Cha** 13

Base Atk +7; **CMB** +5; **CMD** 22

Feats Augment Summoning, Combat Casting, Craft Wondrous Item, Dodge, Scribe Scroll, Skill Focus (Use Magic Device), Spell Focus (conjuration), Toughness, Weapon Finesse

Skills Climb +3, Craft (alchemy) +17, Knowledge (arcana) +21, Knowledge (planes) +21, Perception +18, Sense Motive +14, Spellcraft +21, Stealth +27, Use Magic Device +11; **Racial Modifiers** +4 Climb, +4 Perception, +4 Stealth

Languages Aklo, Common, Dark Folk, Draconic, Giant, Shadowtongue

SQ arcane bond (*amulet of natural armor +2*), magical knack, poison use, soul harvest, summoner's charm (4 rounds)

Combat Gear black smear poison (2 doses; *Pathfinder RPG Bestiary* 54), *potion of bear's endurance*; **Other Gear** mwk kukri, *amulet of natural armor +2*, *headband of vast intelligence +4* (grants ranks in Perception and Sense Motive), spell component pouch, spellbook (contains all prepared spells plus 2d4 additional spells), diamond dust (worth 500 gp)

F5. Northern Watchtower (CR 7)

This tower contains four ballistae, only two of which can be trained on area **F1**.

Creatures: Six dark creepers guard this tower and keep a careful eye out for intruders. Loyal to the Reborn and afraid of punishment for failure, they fight to the death.

DARK CREEPERS (6)	CR 2

XP 600 each

hp 19 each (*Pathfinder RPG Bestiary* 53)

F6. Temple Entrance (CR 10)

The stone surface of the gigantic pillar is pierced here by a cavernous archway, forty feet high and twenty-five feet wide. At the rear of the archway is a massive double door, made from a pair of slabs of dark gray stone reinforced with great riveted

bands of iron. Standing before these doors is a portcullis of thick, black iron bars.

The doors to the temple are stone, just like those in the rest of the complex, but these are 8 inches thick and bolted shut from the other side (hardness 8, hp 120, break DC 28, Disable Device DC 30). The portcullis is constructed of cold iron and is currently lowered (hardness 10, hp 60, lift or break DC 32); the winch in area **F7b** is most often used to raise it.

The doors connect the outer courtyard (area **F1**) to the inner courtyard (area **F9**).

Creatures: Two dark champion guards are posted in front of the gate but behind the portcullis, which provides them cover from attacks. They are accompanied by an owb sorcerer named Solestenes. Solestenes interrogates anyone arriving who claims to have business in the temple using *detect thoughts*; he knows no such visitors are expected and is therefore highly suspicious of anyone claiming to have authorization to enter. These guards are ordered to hold the gate against intruders; Solestenes attacks with his spells while the dark champions use their crossbows until opponents breach the portcullis.

SOLESTENES	CR 9

XP 6,400

Male owb sorcerer 6 (*Pathfinder RPG Bestiary 4* 210)

NE Medium outsider (extraplanar)

Init +11; **Senses** darkvision 90 ft., see in darkness; Perception +14

DEFENSE

AC 23, touch 19, flat-footed 15 (+1 deflection, +7 Dex, +1 dodge, +4 shield)

hp 127 (14 HD; 6d6+8d10+62); fast healing 2

Fort +12, **Ref** +11, **Will** +12

Immune cold

Weaknesses light sensitivity

OFFENSE

Speed 5 ft., fly 60 ft. (perfect)

Melee 2 claws +18 (1d8+7 plus 1d6 cold)

Ranged burning cold +18 touch (3d6 cold)

Special Attacks burning cold, curse of darkness

Spell-Like Abilities (CL 8th; concentration +15)

Constant—*blur*

At will—*deeper darkness*, *detect thoughts* (DC 19), *dust of twilight*^APG (DC 19)

5/day—*shadow step*^UM

1/day—*plane shift* (self only, to or from Shadow Plane only)

Sorcerer Spell-Like Abilities (CL 6th; concentration +13)

10/day—*shadowstrike* (1d4+3 nonlethal plus dazzled)

Sorcerer Spells Known (CL 6th; concentration +13)

3rd (5/day)—*excruciating deformation*^UM (DC 20)

2nd (7/day)—*create pit*^APG (DC 19), *darkvision*, *mirror image*

1st (8/day)—*flare burst*^APG (DC 18), *magic missile*, *ray of enfeeblement* (DC 18), *shield*, *vanish*^APG

0 (at will)—*arcane mark, bleed* (DC 17), *detect magic, ghost sound* (DC 17), *mage hand, prestidigitation, touch of fatigue* (DC 17)
Bloodline shadow^APG

TACTICS

Before Combat Solestenes casts *shield* and *mirror image*.
During Combat Solestenes relies on offensive spells to whittle down opponents from a distance, using burning cold and *excruciating deformation* against opponents within reach.
Morale If reduced below 60 hit points or if the gates to area **F9** are breached, Solestenes casts *shadow step* to retreat and prepares to make a final stand in area **F10**.
Base Statistics Without *shield*, Solestenes's statistics are **AC** 19, touch 19, flat-footed 11.

STATISTICS

Str 22, **Dex** 25, **Con** 19, **Int** 13, **Wis** 13, **Cha** 24
Base Atk +11; **CMB** +17; **CMD** 36
Feats Combat Casting, Combat Expertise, Dodge, Eschew Materials, Flyby Attack, Improved Initiative, Persuasive, Point-Blank Shot

Skills Bluff +20, Diplomacy +24, Fly +22, Intimidate +9, Knowledge (arcana, planes) +12, Perception +14, Sense Motive +12, Spellcraft +12, Stealth +18
Languages Dark Folk (can't speak); telepathy 100 ft.
SQ bloodline arcana (gain bonus on Stealth checks)
Gear *amulet of mighty fists +1, headband of alluring charisma +2, ring of protection +1*

DARK CHAMPIONS (2)	CR 5

XP 1,600 each
hp 59 each (see page 60)

F7. Defensive Balconies (CR 8)

Each of these balconies is 40 feet above the courtyard and has two ballistae. A long-ago earthquake collapsed the tunnel east of area **F7b**, so now the defenders use a long rope made of woven fungal fibers to access the courtyard below. Area **F7b** also contains an old winch to raise or lower the portcullis in the temple entrance (area **F6**), which takes 1 minute.

Creatures: Two cave giants loyal to the dragon Thelamistos, one each occupies either balcony. One attacks with the ballista while the other throws rocks from a large pile of debris. Because of their size, the giants take only a –2 penalty to fire a ballista. These giants have been ordered to remain at their posts and fight to the death.

CAVE GIANT DEFENDERS (2)	CR 6

XP 2,400 each
hp 67 each (*Pathfinder RPG Bestiary 3* 127)

F8. Acolyte's Entrance (CR 6)

This double door is locked and bolted shut from the inside (hardness 8, hp 30, break DC 28, Disable Device DC 30).

Creature: A single surly kyton stands guard here, under orders to let no one enter the temple via this entrance. The kyton extends this prohibition even to the caligni defenders of the temple, and it steps aside only for an owb or for Nephenie. The kyton recently killed a dark creeper attempting to sneak off duty, and it's still trying to pick the tatters of the creature's greasy rags out of its chains.

Cave Giant Defender

KYTON	CR 6

XP 2,400
hp 60 (*Pathfinder RPG Bestiary* 185)

INTRODUCTION

CHAPTER 1:
REMNANTS OF THE DARK

CHAPTER 2:
GAME OF SHADOWS

CHAPTER 3:
FATE OF THE FORSAKEN

APPENDIX 1:
LYRUDRADA

APPENDIX 2:
BESTIARY

F9. Inner Courtyard (CR 13 and CR 10)

A vast inner courtyard hollowed out of the stone column rises to a height of eighty feet overhead. Four freestanding columns of dark stone thirty feet high stand in the center of the room, glimmering with a strange violet light. To the east and west are two dark pools filled to the brim with inky liquid. A sixty-foot-wide archway leads north, and a twenty-five-foot-wide archway leads south; both are surrounded by carvings of enormous spectral figures in dark robes. The eastern alcove of this room appears unfinished, and a dark opening twenty feet in diameter leads into a tunnel of unworked stone.

This inner courtyard was once used by the Forsaken's faithful to prepare for their religious services. The four columns are made of seamless obsidian and were once used in rituals that are now long forgotten. The pools hold clear water only a few feet deep, but as the tiles in the pools are made of shiny obsidian, they make the water appear dark and exceptionally deep.

The south arch leads to the outer courtyard (area **F1**) while the north arch leads to the promenade (area **F10**). The opening to the east leads to the unworked passages that the umbral dragon Thelamistos uses as his lair (area **F11**).

Creature: One of the few creatures in the Forsaken Fane that reports to Veilisendri directly, the umbral dragon Thelamistos came to support the ascendant owb prophet a few months ago. Thelamistos brought a small clan of cave giants that serve him loyally, and the giants now supplement the Reborn's forces.

Thelamistos perches atop one of the carvings on the northern archway, 50 feet above the floor, where the shadows are deep enough for him to hide. If he has any warning that the PCs are present in the Forsaken Fane, he also casts *invisibility*. He swoops down to the PCs whenever he feels that his appearance will cause the most terror and he can catch as many as possible in his breath weapon.

THELAMISTOS	CR 13

XP 25,600

Male young adult umbral dragon (*Pathfinder RPG Bestiary 2* 102)

CE Huge dragon (extraplanar)

Init +4; **Senses** dragon senses; Perception +22

Aura frightful presence (150 ft., DC 21)

DEFENSE

AC 30, touch 8, flat-footed 30 (+4 armor, +18 natural, –2 size)

hp 187 (15d12+90)

Fort +15, **Ref** +9, **Will** +13

Defensive Abilities negative energy affinity; **DR** 5/magic; **Immune** cold, death effects, negative energy, paralysis, sleep; **SR** 24

OFFENSE

Speed 40 ft., fly 200 ft. (poor)

Melee bite +20 (2d8+10/19–20), 2 claws +20 (2d6+7), tail slap +18 (2d6+10), 2 wings +18 (1d8+3)

Space 15 ft.; **Reach** 10 ft. (15 ft. with bite)

Special Attacks breath weapon (50-ft. cone, 10d8 negative energy, Reflex DC 23 half), crush (Small, DC 23, 2d8+10)

Spell-Like Abilities (CL 15th; concentration +19)

At will—*darkness, vampiric touch*

Sorcerer Spells Known (CL 5th; concentration +9)

2nd (5/day)—*bear's endurance, invisibility*

1st (7/day)—*charm person* (DC 15), *cure light wounds, mage armor, ray of enfeeblement* (DC 15)

0 (at will)—*bleed* (DC 14), *detect magic, mage hand, message, open/close, read magic*

TACTICS

Before Combat Before entering battle, Thelamistos casts *bear's endurance, invisibility,* and *mage armor.*

During Combat Thelamistos uses his breath weapon as often as possible, taking to the air to use his melee attacks from beyond the PCs' reach until his breath weapon recharges.

Morale If reduced to fewer than 100 hit points, Thelamistos retreats to area **F11** and calls for aid, as described in Development below.

Base Statistics Without *bear's endurance* and *mage armor,* Thelamistos's statistics are **AC** 26, touch 8, flat-footed 26; **hp** 157; **Fort** +13.

STATISTICS

Str 25, **Dex** 10, **Con** 23, **Int** 18, **Wis** 19, **Cha** 18

Base Atk +15; **CMB** +24; **CMD** 34 (38 vs. trip)

Feats Hover, Improved Critical (bite), Improved Initiative, Multiattack, Power Attack, Skill Focus (Stealth), Snatch, Vital Strike

Skills Bluff +22, Diplomacy +22, Fly +10, Knowledge (arcana, local, planes) +22, Perception +22, Sense Motive +22, Spellcraft +22, Stealth +16

Languages Common, Dark Folk, Draconic, Undercommon

SQ ghost bane, umbral scion

Development: If Thelamistos retreats, he first roars to summon reinforcements. Two cave giants from area **F11** arrive the following round, and two more cave giants arrive the round after that (no more than four cave giants come to Thelamistos's call). As the cave giants arrive, Thelamistos retreats to area **F11**, flying above them. He then heals himself and waits to ambush PCs who intrude on his lair. The cave giants do their best to prevent the PCs from immediately following Thelamistos.

The cave giants are careful to step over the tripwire that triggers the trap in the entrance to area **F11**, which the PCs can note by succeeding at a DC 20 Perception or Sense Motive check.

F10. Promenade (CR 8)

A coffered, vaulted ceiling rises sixty feet overhead above the ornate arabesques of the paired pillars that rise to support it. At the room's center stands a circular well of dark water. Between each pair of pillars and along the room's northern

wall, curtains of gray, phosphorescent webs extend up to the coffered vaults.

Three stone doors, set into large alcoves, lead out to the east side of the room and three to the west, while an enormous archway opens to the south. A stone double door at the north end of the room is visible through the sheets of webbing.

This ancient gathering hall is covered with penumbral webs throughout its northern end. Creatures passing between any of the four pairs of pillars contact the penumbral webs, as do any creatures leaving this room through the double door to the north (to area **F23**).

The webs don't block any other doorways leading out of this room. The pool here is identical to those in area **F9**.

Creatures: The webs in the high ceiling have been colonized by three advanced gloomwings. These large mothlike creatures are immune to the effects of the webs and generally content to let creatures pass below. If any creatures remain in this room for more than 1 minute, however, the gloomwings attack. A gloomwing reduced to fewer than 25 hit points retreats to the ceiling and attempts to remain out of sight among the penumbral webs.

Either of the two owbs the PCs encountered previously may be here, prepared to make a final stand against the PCs. Xhamila and Solestenes can be found here if they escaped from area **E7** or area **F6**, respectively. If so, the gloomwings are already stirred up and attack the PCs as soon as they enter; as long as an owb is present, the gloomwings fight to the death. The owbs remain near the ceiling, using ranged spells against the PCs.

ADVANCED GLOOMWINGS (3) CR 5
XP 1,600 each
hp 47 each (*Pathfinder RPG Bestiary 2* 292, 133)

F11. Dragon's Lair (CR 8 and CR 10)

The rough stone entrances to this chamber (leading from areas **F9** and **F23**) are trapped, as described in Traps; the passage to area **F23** also contains several penumbral webs created by the nimbral child in area **F24**.

Unlike the rest of the temple, this area has the look of crude excavation; its walls appear to be a mixture of rough mining and broken rubble buttressed with mortared stacks. The ceiling varies in height from forty to sixty feet and consists of broken stone slabs, cracked in some long-ago cave-in. In the center of the cavern stands a ten-foot-tall dais constructed from mortared stone, flanked by freestanding columns supporting wide curtains of shimmering black silk. The northern end of the cavern is further adorned by a collection of gray webs that shimmer slightly.

Veilisendri allowed the umbral dragon Thelamistos and his loyal cave giants to lair in this area of the temple, which partially collapsed in an earthquake long ago. Thelamistos believes this area is crude and lacks the grandeur he deserves, so he has set his minions to work

Thelamistos

INTRODUCTION

CHAPTER 1:
REMNANTS OF THE DARK

CHAPTER 2:
GAME OF SHADOWS

CHAPTER 3:
FATE OF THE FORSAKEN

APPENDIX 1:
LYRUDRADA

APPENDIX 2:
BESTIARY

at excavating the rubble and making the lair truly something fitting to his ego.

As the north exit from this room (to area **F23**) is choked with penumbral webs, neither Thelamistos nor his giants use that entrance; they instead come and go through the inner courtyard (area **F9**).

Traps: A trip wire at each of the rough cavern entrances connects to a loose section of the cavern ceiling directly above. If tugged, the wires release thousands of pounds of broken rubble in a 15-foot-by-15-foot area centered on the trip wire.

COLLAPSING CEILING TRAPS (2)	CR 8

XP 4,800 each

Type mechanical; **Perception** DC 23; **Disable Device** DC 20

EFFECTS

Trigger location; **Reset** repair

Effect Atk +15 melee (8d6); multiple targets (all targets in a 15-ft. square)

Creatures: Although this area is Thelamistos's lair, the dragon usually keeps an eye on the inner courtyard (area **F9**) instead. Six cave giants reside in the western half of this room, with large rocks for stools and smelly rags for bedding. Unless called to fight, the cave giants are expanding the walls of this area, chipping away at the stone with their axes and tearing aside rubble with their bare hands. They fight to the death to defend their lair.

CAVE GIANTS (6)	CR 6

XP 2,400 each

hp 67 each (*Pathfinder RPG Bestiary 3* 127)

Treasure: Thelamistos keeps his hoard in an alcove beneath the central dais. A PC who succeeds at a DC 25 Perception check notes that the dais has been recently moved; if viewed from the eastern side (where Thelamistos lairs), this DC is only 15. Recovering the hoard requires moving the heavy dais aside (which requires a successful DC 25 Strength check) or a few hours of digging. The hoard consists of a *potion of remove disease*, an *oil of daylight*, a *ring of spell knowledge II*^{UE}, a *scroll of animate dead*, a *belt of foraging*^{UE}, a marble bust of a duergar king worth 300 gp, a broken platinum holy symbol of Alazhra worth 400 gp, a gold plate inset with jade and engraved with images of drow and spiders worth 685 gp, 3,452 cp, 1,424 sp, 104 gp, and 17 pp.

F12. Trophy Hall (CR 9)

This chamber appears to have been thoroughly looted long ago, as it contains only dusty plinths, broken display cases, and forlorn portions of wall-mounted skulls. Water dribbles down the south wall from a crack in the ceiling, and an alcove to the south contains a profusion of fungus that nearly obscures

a stone door at the rear of the alcove. Other doors lead to the north and east.

Once a trophy hall for the followers of the Forsaken, this chamber was thoroughly looted by Haramil's forces long ago. The Reborn know of the creatures lairing here and have thus far avoided the chamber.

Hazard: A large patch of brown mold grows among the fungus in the southern alcove, covering the 10-foot-square area in front of the door leading to area **F13**.

Creatures: Lurking in the fungi are two moldwretches, Orph and Ubdro, that are bonded with the brown mold. They dislike intruders and are unfriendly to other creatures. The moldwretches initially hope that anyone entering this chamber simply leaves without disturbing them. If discovered, they gruffly insist that they want to be left alone. If the PCs establish a rapport with these creatures despite their surly nature, they can provide information about the Reborn forces in area **F15**. They don't know about any other denizens of the Forsaken Fane, as they haven't left this room. If the PCs disturb the moldwretches' fungus lair or harm their brown mold, they attack immediately.

MOLDWRETCHES (2)	CR 7

XP 3,200 each

hp 85 each (*Pathfinder RPG Bestiary 6* 191)

F13. Trapped Chamber (CR 8)

This bare chamber has a steep set of stairs that lead up to the west. A double door to the north sits in a shallow alcove, as does a door to the east.

The east door leading to the trophy hall (area **F12**) is noticeably colder than the stone around it, due to the brown mold on the other side. Anyone who examines this room and succeeds at a DC 12 Perception check notes that smears of grime indicate that all recent traffic through this room uses the stairs and the north door.

Creature: Although the double door seems the safest, this is only because the ooze lairing there has been trained to ignore Reborn troops moving through it. This ooze currently takes the form of wall scythe trap clinging to the interior of the alcove around the north door.

DEATHTRAP OOZE	CR 8

XP 4,800

hp 126 (*Pathfinder RPG Bestiary 3* 64)

Trap: The deathtrap ooze takes the form of a trap that releases a deadly, double-bladed scythe as soon as anyone steps within 5 feet of the north door. The scythe swings down and then up, attacking its target twice. As the Reborn forces keep the trap well fed, it doesn't attack any creature that resembles a caligni, an owb, or a shadow mastiff; it triggers for any other type of creature.

DOUBLE-BLADED SCYTHE TRAP	CR 8

XP —

Type mechanical; **Perception** DC 28; **Disable Device** DC 23

EFFECTS

Trigger location; **Reset** automatic (1 round)
Effect Atk +20/+20 melee (2d4+6/×4)

F14. Guarded Landing (CR 8)

This wide landing connects stairs up to the temple's exterior defenses to stairs leading down to the chambers occupied by the Reborn forces. It is otherwise bare.

Creatures: A Reborn commando and a shadow mastiff guard this landing at all times. The Reborn forces are accustomed to the shadow mastiff's baying and are unaffected by it, but the noise alerts the Reborn in areas **F15** and **F16** to intruders coming from this direction.

REBORN COMMANDO	CR 7

XP 3,200

hp 91 (see page 22)

SHADOW MASTIFF	CR 5

XP 1,600

hp 51 (*Pathfinder RPG Bestiary 3* 241)

F15. Mustering Hall (CR 10)

This large, odd-shaped hall contains mounds of garbage and charred remains of old cook fires strewn upon the floor. A few bedrolls are carelessly folded and stacked against one wall. Large pillars support the room's ceiling, and a ladder leans against one of them. Frescoes in the ceiling are almost entirely obscured by soot from previous fires in this room. A wide hallway leads out of this room to the north, and narrow doors exit to the west, south, and east.

This room was once a gathering area, and the frescoes showed scenes of caligni cowering in terror before cloaked and shadowy giants. The main force of the Reborn camped in this room, and even a cursory search shows that over two dozen soldiers were once billeted here.

Creatures: Only a few caligni remain in this room, along with a shadow mastiff watchdog. Ordered to clean up this room and scrub the ceiling, the occupants haven't done much more than push the trash into piles and acquire a ladder to reach the stained frescoes above. Unless warned of intruders—such as the baying of shadow mastiffs in area **F14** or **F17** or the sounds of combat from area **F10**—these troops don't expect trouble and are likely easy to surprise. If alerted to trespassers, they hide amid the detritus of the room and prepare an ambush. Eager to demonstrate their devotion by fighting rather than cleaning, these troops neither retreat nor surrender.

REBORN CUTTHROATS (2)	CR 7

XP 3,200 each

hp 81 each (see page 24)

DARK CREEPERS (3)	CR 2

XP 600 each

hp 19 each (*Pathfinder RPG Bestiary* 53)

SHADOW MASTIFF	CR 5

XP 1,600

hp 51 (*Pathfinder RPG Bestiary 3* 241)

Treasure: Some of the former residents here were dispatched to other parts of Lyrudrada with no chance to recover their personal valuables. A thorough search uncovers a crimson tourmaline worth 160 gp and a total of 54 gp.

F16. Officer Barracks (CR 10)

This plain chamber holds rows of old stone bunks, many shrouded in a thick layer of dust. A few of the bunks appear to have been recently cleaned off. Doors lead out of this room in several directions.

Just as several rank-and-file members of the Reborn were once billeted in area **F15**, leaders were billeted here.

Creatures: Currently occupying this chamber is the cult's guard captain—an owb named Unom—and two dark champions serving as his adjutants. If alerted to intruders, one dark champion leaves to bring the shadow mastiffs in area **F17** into this room to bolster their defense. Dedicated and disciplined, the residents of this room attempt to defeat any intruders at all costs.

UNOM	CR 9

XP 6,400

Male owb fighter 3 (*Pathfinder RPG Bestiary 4* 210)
NE Medium outsider (extraplanar)
Init +10; **Senses** darkvision 60 ft., see in darkness; Perception +18

DEFENSE

AC 22, touch 15, flat-footed 17 (+7 armor, +4 Dex, +1 dodge)
hp 118 (11d10+58); fast healing 2
Fort +14, **Ref** +9, **Will** +11 (+1 vs. fear)
Immune cold
Weaknesses light sensitivity

OFFENSE

Speed 5 ft., fly 40 ft. (perfect)
Melee 2 claws +19 (2d6+7 plus 1d6 cold)
Ranged burning cold +17 touch (3d6 cold)
Special Attacks burning cold, curse of darkness

INTRODUCTION

CHAPTER 1:
REMNANTS OF THE DARK

CHAPTER 2:
GAME OF SHADOWS

CHAPTER 3:
FATE OF THE FORSAKEN

APPENDIX 1:
LYRUDRADA

APPENDIX 2:
BESTIARY

Spell-Like Abilities (CL 8th; concentration +10)
Constant—*blur*
At will—*deeper darkness, detect thoughts* (DC 14), *dust of twilight*APG (DC 14)
5/day—*shadow step*UM
1/day—*plane shift* (self only, to or from Shadow Plane only)

TACTICS

During Combat Unom casts *deeper darkness* and *shadow step* to reach vulnerable-looking opponents with his claw attacks, using Power Attack if they seem easy to strike.
Morale Unom fights to the death.

STATISTICS

Str 24, **Dex** 22, **Con** 21, **Int** 13, **Wis** 19, **Cha** 14
Base Atk +11; **CMB** +18; **CMD** 35
Feats Combat Reflexes, Dodge, Flyby Attack, Improved Initiative, Improved Natural Attack (claw), Point-Blank Shot, Power Attack, Weapon Focus (claw)
Skills Bluff +11, Diplomacy +10, Fly +19, Intimidate +16, Knowledge (planes) +12, Perception +18, Sense Motive +15, Spellcraft +8, Stealth +15
Languages Dark Folk (can't speak); telepathy 100 ft.
SQ armor training 1
Gear *+1 breastplate, pale blue rhomboid ioun stone*

DARK CHAMPIONS (2)	CR 5

XP 1,600 each
hp 59 each (see page 60)

Treasure: Hidden beneath one of the unused bunks (Perception DC 22 to notice) is a pouch with 512 gp, two topazes worth 450 gp each, and a sapphire worth 1,100 gp.

F17. Armory (CR 7)

This chamber was once an armory, but it has long been stripped bare of anything of value or use. Some dried river reeds on the floor provide a modicum of comfort to the room's inhabitants, particularly the alcoves sheltered by tattered curtains. The two obvious doors lead to the officer's barracks (area **F16**). A secret door leading to area **F19** can be located with a successful DC 22 Perception check; the Reborn don't know about it.

Creatures: The Reborn use this room as a kennel. The two shadow mastiffs here eagerly attack intruders and bay if they hear the sounds of combat nearby. A shadow mastiff reduced to fewer than 15 hit points flees.

SHADOW MASTIFFS (2)	CR 5

XP 1,600 each
hp 51 each (*Pathfinder RPG Bestiary 3* 241)

F18. Shadow Temple (CR 10)

The walls of this large room contain several smashed bas-relief carvings of smoke, hooded cloaks, and grasping claws. A double row of columns supports a domed ceiling eighty feet above. An alcove to the northeast holds the base of a broken statue, but atop this jagged base stands a metal frame with a piece of black, scaly hide stretched across it. A purple-flamed candle behind the framed hide throws vast shadow across the room. Two lidded urns of black stone stand in front of this altar.

Once a temple to the Forsaken, this area has been reconsecrated to the owb prophet Veilisendri. Worship remains sporadic among the Reborn for now, but with Veilisendri's anticipated apotheosis at hand, the two priests here are working to get things ready for formal services.

As long as the strange canvas gives off its shadow, an *unhallow* effect fills this room. The *unhallow* has a secondary effect providing *freedom of movement* to adherents of Veilisendri: the adherents' shadows seem to move and flow, granting them a supernatural ability to slip out of impediments. If the candle is extinguished or the frame is destroyed (hardness 5, hp 15, break DC 20), the *unhallow* effect immediately ends but a spiritual backlash occurs; see Development on page 50.

Creatures: The temple is tended by two dark caller priests named Otishesk and Shadriev. If the priests are aware of intruders, they attempt to uncover or knock over the urns near the altar (a move action for each); doing so releases the trained slithering trackers stored inside. Both the priests and the oozes fight to the death.

DARK CALLER PRIESTS (2)	CR 8

XP 4,800 each
Dark caller cleric of Veilisendri 6 (*Pathfinder RPG Bestiary 4* 42)
NE Medium humanoid (dark folk)
Init +5; **Senses** *detect magic*, see in darkness; Perception +15

DEFENSE

AC 24, touch 15, flat-footed 19 (+4 armor, +4 Dex, +1 dodge, +3 natural, +2 shield)
hp 97 each (14d8+34)
Fort +9, **Ref** +13, **Will** +12
Weaknesses light blindness

OFFENSE

Speed 30 ft.
Melee *+1 ominous dagger* +16/+11 (1d4+5/19–20)
Special Attacks channel negative energy 8/day (DC 18, 3d6), death throes, sneak attack +2d6
Spell-Like Abilities (CL 8th; concentration +13)
Constant—*detect magic*
At will—*bleed* (DC 16)
3/day—*deeper darkness, shadow step*UM
1/day—*shadow conjuration* (DC 19)
Cleric Spell-Like Abilities (CL 6th; concentration +10)
7/day—*touch of darkness* (3 rounds), *touch of evil* (3 rounds)
Cleric Spells Prepared (CL 6th; concentration +10)
3rd—*cure serious wounds, deeper darkness*D, *dispel magic, stone shape*

2nd—*blindness/deafness* (blindness only)^D (DC 17), *cure moderate wounds*, *death knell* (DC 17), *hold person* (DC 16), *spiritual weapon*

1st—*command* (DC 15), *cure light wounds* (2), *obscuring mist*^{D}, *sanctuary* (DC 15)

0 (at will)—*bleed* (DC 14), *detect magic*, *read magic*, *virtue*

D domain spell; **Domains** Darkness, Evil

Otishesk

TACTICS

During Combat The priests cast *deeper darkness* to disorient and ambush their foes. They prefer to capture enemies, using spells such as *hold person* and *blindness/deafness* so they can later sacrifice their foes to Veilisendri.

Morale The fanatical priests defend the temple with their lives.

STATISTICS

Str 19, **Dex** 19, **Con** 12, **Int** 13, **Wis** 18, **Cha** 20

Base Atk +10; **CMB** +14; **CMD** 29

Feats Blind-Fight, Combat Casting, Craft Magic Arms and Armor, Dodge, Intimidating Prowess, Selective Channeling, Spell Focus (necromancy), Toughness

Skills Climb +8, Intimidate +24, Knowledge (religion) +11, Perception +15, Spellcraft +11, Stealth +16; **Racial Modifiers** +4 Climb, +4 Perception, +4 Stealth

Languages Dark Folk, Undercommon

SQ poison use, shadow ritual

Combat Gear black smear (2 doses; *Pathfinder RPG Bestiary* 54); **Other Gear** *+2 leather armor*, *+1 buckler*, *+1 ominous*^{UE} *dagger*, *cloak of resistance +1*, spell component pouch, obsidian holy symbol worth 50 gp

SLITHERING TRACKERS (2)   **CR 4**

XP 1,200 each

hp 42 each (*Pathfinder RPG Bestiary 2* 250)

Development: If the *unhallow* effect in this room ends, the shadowy powers that Veilisendri draws upon take notice. The space in front of the altar swirls with dark energy, and after 1 round, a multitentacled horror of menacing darkness and shifting shadows appears in the nearest open space before the altar. Treat this creature as a summoned shadow roper (*Pathfinder RPG Bestiary 4* 238) that disappears after 2d4 rounds. During this time, it lashes out at all creatures in the room, including any surviving priests and slithering trackers.

F19. High Priestess's Quarters (CR 11)

Cracked and defaced murals in myriad shades of gray adorn the walls of this chamber. The broken bases of statues stand in two alcoves amid a mound of shattered stone. In the center of the room lie a threadbare blanket, a copper pitcher, and a clay bowl.

The ancient high priest's quarters was thoroughly sacked in Haramil's raid. Nephenie has since taken up residence here and has done nothing to refurbish the chamber other than bring in some simple personal items. She spends most of her time here meditating on the Forsaken, leaving day-to-day administration of the Reborn to underlings while she seeks spiritual enlightenment.

The PCs can locate the secret door to area **F17** with a successful DC 28 Perception check; Nephenie isn't aware of its existence.

INTRODUCTION

CHAPTER 1:
REMNANTS OF THE DARK

CHAPTER 2:
GAME OF SHADOWS

CHAPTER 3:
FATE OF THE FORSAKEN

APPENDIX 1:
LYRUDRADA

APPENDIX 2:
BESTIARY

Creature: Nephenie remains in this chamber in communion with her inner voices and does not leave unless summoned by Veilisendri. If warned of intruders by the priests in **F18**, she sends them back to their post and prepares for combat alone. Nephenie's chalky skin has become even more pale as the shadowbound corruption overtakes her, and very little rouses her to any emotion except pain and religious fervor.

NEPHENIE	CR 11

XP 12,800

Female caligni oracle 12 (*Pathfinder RPG Bestiary 5* 66, *Pathfinder RPG Advanced Player's Guide* 42)

NE Medium humanoid (dark folk)

Init +6; **Senses** darkvision 60 ft., see in darkness; Perception +3

DEFENSE

AC 24, touch 12, flat-footed 22 (+8 armor, +2 Dex, +4 shield)

hp 153 (12d8+96)

Fort +13, **Ref** +9, **Will** +12

Weaknesses light sensitivity; **SR** 23

OFFENSE

Speed 30 ft.

Melee *dagger of venom* +11/+6 (1d4+2/19–20)

Special Attacks death throes

Spell-Like Abilities (CL 12th, concentration +17)

1/day—*shadow conjuration* (2nd-level spells only; DC 19)

Oracle Spells Known (CL 12th; concentration +17)

6th (3/day)—*heal, greater heroism, mass cure moderate wounds*

5th (5/day)—*mass cure light wounds, plane shift* (DC 20), *spell resistance, telekinesis* (DC 20)

4th (7/day)—*air walk, cure critical wounds, freedom of movement, spiritual ally*^APG, *unholy blight* (DC 19)

3rd (7/day)—*blindness/deafness* (DC 18), *cure serious wounds, dispel magic, heroism, magic vestment, speak with dead* (DC 18)

2nd (7/day)—*aid, bear's endurance, cure moderate wounds, death knell* (DC 17), *hold person* (DC 17), *levitate, minor image* (DC 17), *silence* (DC 17), *spiritual weapon*

1st (7/day)—*command* (DC 16), *cure light wounds, divine favor, forbid action*^UM (DC 16), *ray of sickening*^UM (DC 16), *sanctuary* (DC 16), *unseen servant*

0 (at will)—*bleed* (DC 15), *create water, detect magic, detect poison, ghost sound* (DC 15), *guidance, mage hand, mending, read magic, resistance, stabilize*

Mystery ancestor^UM

TACTICS

Before Combat Nephenie casts extended *magic vestment* early each day and uses her spirit shield revelation. If she suspects combat is imminent, she casts *air walk, bear's endurance, freedom of movement,* and *spell resistance.*

During Combat Nephenie attempts to remain out of melee and uses her ranged spells and storm of souls revelation to defeat her foes. If in melee, she casts a quickened *divine favor* and uses her spirit of the warrior revelation.

Morale Nephenie is a fanatic and fights to the death, but if reduced to fewer than 60 hit points she retreats just long enough heal herself and renew her attack.

Base Statistics Without Nephenie's preparatory spells and effects, her statistics are **AC** 13, touch 12, flat-footed 11; **hp** 129; **Fort** +11; **Con** 18.

STATISTICS

Str 13, **Dex** 14, **Con** 22, **Int** 8, **Wis** 8, **Cha** 20

Base Atk +9; **CMB** +10; **CMD** 22

Feats Craft Wondrous Item, Extend Spell, Improved Initiative, Iron Will, Quicken Spell, Toughness

Skills Knowledge (history) +14, Knowledge (religion) +14, Perception +3, Spellcraft +14, Stealth +6

Languages Common, Dark Folk

SQ oracle's curse (haunted), revelations (spirit of the warrior^UM, spirit shield^UM, storm of souls^UM, wisdom of the ancestors^UM), shadowbound corruption^HA (stage 3, manifestation level 3, eerie perception, emptiness of the void, weaver of lies)

Gear mwk buckler, *dagger of venom, cloak of resistance +3, headband of alluring charisma +4,* spell component pouch, obsidian holy symbol worth 50 gp

F20. Shadow Font (CR 8)

A small fountain burbles from an elaborate carving into a shallow basin at the west end of this hall. The pitch-black water seems to absorb light. Wisps of gray webbing cling to the walls and ceiling. Doors stand in alcoves along the north and south walls of this hall, and the hall's east end opens into a larger hallway running north and south.

The webs in this hall are penumbral webs created by the nimbral child in area **F24**. The font at the western end of the hall contains a tiny opening to the Shadow Plane, which expels inky water drawn from that realm. The water never overflows the basin and refills it immediately if any water is removed. The water deals 2d6 points of negative energy damage and 1 point of Strength damage to creatures that touch it; a creature who succeeds at a DC 17 Fortitude save halves the negative energy damage and negates the Strength damage. Although the water deals negative energy damage, it does not heal undead. Water removed from the basin evaporates after 1 hour.

Creature: A bodak called forth from the Shadow Plane lurks in this hall and attacks anyone who is not a member of the Reborn. It attempts to affect as many PCs as possible with its death gaze and fights until destroyed.

BODAK	CR 8

XP 4,800

hp 85 (*Pathfinder RPG Bestiary 2* 48)

Development: The sounds of combat here alerts the dark callers from the cultist quarters (area **F21**), who arrive in 1d3 rounds.

F21. Cultist Quarters (CR 8)

Each of these rooms was assigned to members of the Reborn interested in becoming priests of Veilisendri or otherwise aiding Nephenie directly. Each room contains two simple cots and a basin of water.

Creatures: Only the easternmost chamber of these chambers is occupied. The three dark callers here are in training to become priests of Veilisendri. They are currently undergoing a ritual purification involving fasting and meditation, but they are quick to attack intruders. They prefer to summon monsters with *shadow*

Nephenie

conjuration and then close to attack in melee with their poisoned daggers.

DARK CALLERS (3)	CR 5

XP 1,600 each

hp 52 each (*Pathfinder RPG Bestiary 4* 42)

Treasure: A search of these rooms turns up an opal worth 350 gp, an aquamarine worth 500 gp, an ornate silver flute worth 180 gp, and a total of 528 gp.

F22. Forsaken Walk (CR 8)

Once a religious processional, this corridor is now choked with penumbral webs created by the nimbral child in area **F24**. The webs are not thick enough to hinder movement through this area, but any creature that enters a space adjacent to any wall here automatically comes in contact with the penumbral webs. The webs are particularly thick in the alcove at the north end of this hall. In addition, the door to the inner sanctum (area **F26**) is completely concealed by the webs and requires a successful DC 22 Perception check to spot. Even if discovered, the door is bolted shut from the other side (hardness 8, hp 30, break DC 28, Disable Device DC 30).

Creature: A pelagastr protean summoned by Veilisendri lurks incorporeally at the north end of this hall. It is content to remain hidden until discovered, or until anyone spots the hidden door to the inner sanctum. In either event, the pelagastr lunges forth to attack. If reduced to fewer than 20 hit points, it flees through the wall to area **F26**, where Veilisendri promptly destroys it for its failure.

PELAGASTR	CR 8

XP 4,800

hp 105 (*Pathfinder RPG Bestiary 6* 214)

F23. Shadow Door (CR 10)

This wide corridor is shrouded in penumbral webs, like area **F22**. As this hallway is narrower, any creature moving through this hall automatically comes into contact with the penumbral webs. The webs cover the alcove and double door leading to the inner sanctum (area **F26**). Spotting the double door requires a successful DC 22 Perception check, as does spotting the two bodaks standing motionless within the webs in front of the door. As with the other doors to the inner sanctum, these doors are bolted shut (hardness 8, hp 30, break DC 28, Disable Device DC 30).

Creatures: Two bodaks stand in front of the door to area **F26**, completely concealed by the penumbral webs. They attack if discovered.

BODAKS (2)   CR 8

XP 4,800 each

hp 85 each (*Pathfinder RPG Bestiary 2* 48)

F24. Purification Chamber (CR 11)

The original dimensions of this chamber are entirely obscured by layers upon layers of pale-gray webs covering every inch of its walls, floor, and ceiling. The edges of a dry font are barely visible in an alcove at the northern end of the room.

Though this room was once a purification chamber, but the shallow pool in the northern alcove is long dry. Penumbral webs cover every surface and stretch between the walls and floor. Double doors lead east to Nhamino's ritual chamber (area **F25**) and west to the inner sanctum (area **F26**). This door to the inner sanctum is the only entrance that isn't bolted shut, making it the easiest way to reach Veilisendri.

Creature: A nimbral child called forth from the Shadow Plane by Veilisendri now lairs here. It has spent much of its time creating the penumbral webs that shroud many of the rooms in the northern part of the Forsaken Fane; Veilisendri believes these webs, when empowered by the *Cradle of Night*, snare the souls of dead Reborn cultists to fuel his apotheosis. Veilisendri believes that the nimbral child knows more about the Forsaken than it is letting on, but the nimbral child is content to merely spin webs for now.

As soon as the nimbral child identifies intruders in this area, it cloaks the area in *deeper darkness*, casts *spell turning*, and then attempts to obliterate the intruders with its breath weapon and offensive spell-like abilities. One engaged, the nimbral child does not cease its attacks until the PCs leave the fane altogether.

NIMBRAL CHILD   CR 11

XP 12,800

hp 133 (see page 61)

Development: The sounds of combat draw Nhamino from the ritual chamber (area **F25**) to investigate. Rather than join the combat, however, Nhamino merely observes the PCs for 1 round and then withdraws to the ritual chamber to prepare the ambush described in that section.

Once the nimbral child is defeated, the penumbral webbing throughout the Forsaken Fane evaporates.

F25. Ritual Chamber (CR 13)

The southern portion of this chamber is shrouded in pale webs. Several dark humanoid forms hang wrapped within them like flies awaiting a spider. The northern portion of this room is clear of the webs and resembles a sultan's boudoir: cushions, gauzy curtains, ornate side tables, and even a large hookah are all neatly arranged in a shallow alcove.

Once a ritual chamber, this room has been taken over by one of Veilisendri's allies from the Shadow Plane, the dark naga shadow lord Nhamino. Nhamino keeps the northern alcove clear of webs, as it is here that he stores all of the creature comforts he has obtained since arriving in Lyrudrada.

The southern half of the room is covered in penumbral webs, such that anyone entering this room from the hallway through the south must pass through them. Hanging in the webs are the motionless forms of three dark stalkers. Fanatical volunteers willing to give their souls to Veilisendri, each is currently unconscious at –12 hit points, but stable. The dark stalkers are spaced around the room so that the areas of their death throes overlap each other and cover all of this room except the alcove in which Nhamino rests.

Creatures: The dark naga Nhamino has been conducting experiments on penumbral webbing and studying its ability to capture souls. The Reborn volunteers here serve as both part of his experiment and a trap for intruders. As soon as Nhamino identifies intruders in the room, he casts a *magic missile* spell to target the unconscious dark stalkers. The damage is sufficient to kill them, causing a chain reaction of death throes. Once the dark stalkers are slain, their souls immediately manifest as shadows (one greater shadow and two normal shadows) rather than passing on to the Great Beyond. These shadows are wholly obedient to Nhamino and fight until destroyed.

NHAMINO   CR 12

XP 19,200

Male advanced shadow lord dark naga (*Pathfinder RPG Bestiary 4* 238, *Pathfinder RPG Bestiary* 294, 211)

LE Large outsider (augmented aberration)

Init +14; **Senses** darkvision 60 ft., *detect thoughts*, low-light vision, see in darkness; Perception +21

DEFENSE

AC 29, touch 20, flat-footed 18 (+10 Dex, +1 dodge, +9 natural, –1 size)

hp 159 (14d8+96)

Fort +10, **Ref** +14, **Will** +15; +2 vs. charm

Defensive Abilities guarded thoughts, incorporeal step, shadow blend; **DR** 15/magic; **Immune** poison; **Resist** cold 20, electricity 20; **SR** 18

OFFENSE

Speed 40 ft.

Melee bite +19 (1d4+4), sting +19 (2d4+4 plus poison) or touch attack +13 (1d6+4; Fort DC 24 negates)

Space 10 ft.; **Reach** 5 ft.

Special Attacks cloying gloom blast (DC 24)

Spell-Like Abilities (CL 10th; concentration +17)

At will—*ray of sickening*^UM (DC 18)

3/day—*shadow conjuration* (DC 21), *shadow step*^UM

1/day—*greater shadow conjuration* (DC 24), *shadow walk* (DC 22)

INTRODUCTION

CHAPTER 1: REMNANTS OF THE DARK

CHAPTER 2: GAME OF SHADOWS

CHAPTER 3: FATE OF THE FORSAKEN

APPENDIX 1: LYRUDRADA

APPENDIX 2: BESTIARY

Sorcerer Spells Known (CL 7th; concentration +14)

3rd (6/day)—*displacement, lightning bolt* (DC 20)

2nd (8/day)—*false life, mirror image, scorching ray*

1st (8/day)—*expeditious retreat, mage armor, magic missile, ray of enfeeblement* (DC 18), *vanish*^{APG}

0 (at will)—*bleed* (DC 17), *detect magic, mage hand, mending, message, open/close, read magic*

TACTICS

During Combat Nhamino casts *magic missile* to slay the caligni hanging in the webs, as described above. He then fights at range with his spells for as long as possible, relying on his cloying gloom blast to incapacitate enemies that approach him in melee.

Morale If reduced below 20 hit points, Nhamino uses *shadow step* to retreat to area **F26** and fight there alongside Veilisendri.

STATISTICS

Str 18, **Dex** 30, **Con** 22, **Int** 20, **Wis** 19, **Cha** 25

Nhamino

Base Atk +10; **CMB** +15; **CMD** 36 (can't be tripped)

Feats Arcane Strike, Combat Casting, Combat Reflexes, Dodge, Eschew Materials, Improved Initiative, Iron Will, Weapon Finesse

Skills Acrobatics +27, Bluff +21, Diplomacy +13, Disguise +13, Escape Artist +16, Intimidate +21, Knowledge (arcana) +22, Knowledge (planes) +19, Perception +21, Sense Motive +14, Spellcraft +18, Stealth +27

Languages Aklo, Common, Infernal, Shadowtongue, Undercommon

SQ planar thinning

GREATER SHADOW	CR 8

XP 4,800

hp 58 (*Pathfinder RPG Bestiary* 245)

SHADOWS (2)	CR 3

XP 800 each

hp 19 each (*Pathfinder RPG Bestiary* 245)

Treasure: The brass-and-silver hookah is worth 1,200 gp, and the curtains, carpets, and other furnishings are worth a total of 2,500 gp. Concealed beneath the cushions is a *chime of interruption*, a set of four crystal goblets worth 120 gp each, and a darkwood-and-platinum music box worth 4,000 gp.

F26. Inner Sanctum (CR 13)

This large chamber has several carvings that jut from the stone walls, casting erratic shadows around the room. These carvings have all been badly chipped, and the frescoes between them smashed. Four obsidian pillars reach a domed ceiling sixty feet overhead. A circle of pulsing purple light is inscribed on the floor between them, with a fist-sized stone resting at its center. The broken remnant of statues stand in alcoves to the north, flanking a pitch-black pool.

This inner sanctum is the domain of the owb prophet Veilisendri. Although the chamber still shows damage from the days when Haramil and his forces stormed the Forsaken Fane and destroyed its carvings and statues, Veilisendri has restored some of the eldritch power in the ring of runes at the center of this room. The *Cradle of Night* now rests within the runes, empowering the penumbral webs throughout the Forsaken Fane and drawing in the souls of the Reborn cultists across Lyrudrada to fuel Veilisendri's apotheosis. The *Cradle of Night* can't be removed from within the ring of runes as long as Veilisendri lives.

The pool in this room is lined with obsidian, just like the pools in area **F9**. The doors to areas **F22** and **F23** are bolted shut with heavy floor bolts on this side.

Creature: The owb prophet Veilisendri spends all his time here, drawing on energies snared from the souls of the Reborn by the *Cradle of Night*. Veilisendri is concerned that the PCs have penetrated this deeply into the Forsaken Fane, but he arrogantly insists that they have aided his apotheosis by murdering so many loyal members of his cult. Veilisendri hopes that this ruse is sufficient to put the PCs off-guard long enough for him to defeat them.

VEILISENDRI	CR 13

XP 25,600
Male owb prophet
hp 184 (see page 62)

Treasure: The most important treasure here is the *Cradle of Night*, the artifact responsible for the PCs' shadowbound corruption and the only method of removing the corruption. Veilisendri has also hoarded some offerings provided by loyal Reborn cultists, which he keeps behind the broken statue bases at the north edge of the room. This hoard includes a *+2 kukri*, a *ring of the ram*, thin leather *boots of speed*, a *cloak of arachnida*, a platinum carving of a night hag with sapphire eyes worth 3,500 gp, 12,450 gp, and 310 pp.

The Cradle of Night

The enigmatic demigods of the Shadow Plane known as the Forsaken gifted the *Cradles of Night* to the refugees of the long-lost city of Calignos after their flight into the Darklands. The *Cradles of Night* provided great strength, supernaturally extended life spans, and useful manifestations of the shadowbound corruption (*Pathfinder RPG Horror Adventures* 34). But these artifacts were not benevolent gifts; they also bound their owners and their owners' followers to the Forsaken. When those who accepted powers from a *Cradle of Night* died, their bodies vanished in flashes of light as their souls were shunted into the Shadow Plane to infuse the Forsaken with power. In time, the Forsaken hoped to use this accumulated soul energy to enter the Material Plane, but when these mysterious demigods suffered their own unknown cataclysm, the *Cradles of Night* lost the power to shunt souls. Yet the dark folk all retain their explosive death throes—a lasting legacy of their genesis.

The powers presented below are for the artifact as it appears in this adventure—a fraction of the artifact's original powers when the Forsaken still lived. Most notably, the *Cradle of Night* no longer has the ability to transform humanoids into dark folk, although its ability to impart shadowbound corruption remains.

CRADLE OF NIGHT		MAJOR ARTIFACT
SLOT none	**CL** 20th	**WEIGHT** 5 lbs.
AURA strong illusion [evil]		

Once each year, a *Cradle of Night* can infuse a single living creature that handles it with a manifestation of the shadowbound corruption (*Pathfinder RPG Horror Adventures* 34). If the creature wishes to reject the manifestation, it can do so by succeeding at a DC 25 Will save, but if the creature fails this saving throw, it gains the manifestation's stain without its gift. A creature with a manifestation of the shadowbound corruption that carries a *Cradle of Night* on its person ceases aging, gains a +4 profane bonus to Strength and Constitution, and gains fast healing equal to its total Hit Dice. These effects are suppressed whenever the creature is in bright light, but time spent not aging does not catch up to the bearer at such times.

DESTRUCTION

A *Cradle of Night* that is exposed to direct sunlight for 8 consecutive hours becomes relatively fragile and can be destroyed by damage, but spending at least a minute in shadow or darkness removes this fragility. While fragile, a *Cradle of Night* has hardness 15 and 30 hp. If the artifact is destroyed, each creature that has willingly accepted a manifestation from the *Cradle of Night* must succeed at a DC 25 Fortitude save or be immediately destroyed, as if by a *sphere of annihilation*. Creatures that did not willingly gain the *Cradle of Night's* manifestations instead immediately lose the shadowbound corruption (and all manifestations it granted), but suffer no other ill effect.

Concluding the Adventure

With Veilisendri defeated, the Reborn cult quickly falls apart. If Nephenie lives, she might hold the cult together for a short time, but her own emptiness and disillusionment make her an ineffective leader, and her leadership only delays the cult's inevitable dissolution. In any event, the Reborn quickly abandon the Forsaken Fane rather than face the PCs. If the dark dancer rogue Zyler is still shadowing the party (see page 17), he may attempt to steal the *Cradle of Night*; otherwise, the PCs can take the artifact to the surface to destroy it and remove their shadowbound corruption. As the PCs likely did not willingly gain manifestations from the artifact, destroying it poses them no harm.

With the fall of the Reborn, Lyrudrada returns to its usual delicate political balance. Aiyana and any survivors of the Bleakshore Council are extremely grateful to the PCs and offer them each a magic item worth 26,000 gp or less as a reward for their efforts. These can be selected from items listed for sale in the Lyrudrada city stat block (see page 57) or could be tailored to the PCs based on their desires and on their experiences in this adventure. In the future, Lyrudrada can serve as an excellent base camp for the PCs to begin more extensive exploration of the Darklands.

INTRODUCTION

CHAPTER 1:
REMNANTS OF THE DARK

CHAPTER 2:
GAME OF SHADOWS

CHAPTER 3:
FATE OF THE FORSAKEN

APPENDIX 1:
LYRUDRADA

APPENDIX 2:
BESTIARY

Appendix 1

Lyrudrada

Lyrudrada is an ancient caligni city located in Nar-Voth, the uppermost layer of the Darklands. Although the city doesn't lie along any major trade routes and is considered a "cold walk" by many denizens of the Darklands (a term denoting a tunnel that ends at a subterranean river or water-filled cavern), it is nevertheless easy to reach from the Long Walk, the major thoroughfare through Nar-Voth. The Grayfoam River provides access to most districts in Lyrudrada, flowing southeast from duergar river-ports, although the river has a tendency to churn and flood near the city itself, making regular river traffic unreliable. Darklands traders generally prefer to conduct their business in the Shadow Caverns above (*Pathfinder Campaign Setting: Nidal, Land of Shadows* 50) or the city of Sverspume further below (*Pathfinder Chronicles:*

Into the Darklands 42), both of which are more welcoming to trade than the insular city of Lyrudrada. Nevertheless, thousands of caligni call Lyrudrada home, and the city receives some merchant traffic from the back ways of the Darklands, particularly in the district called Traders' Rift.

Lyrudrada is in the middle of a social upheaval stronger than any it has experienced since the human warlord Haramil invaded the city millennia ago. An elite group of dark stalkers and owbs have ruled the delicately balanced system of caste-clans in Lyrudrada for untold generations. With the sudden rise to power of the Reborn—an obscure secret society that few in Lyrudrada ever took seriously— the city has plunged into chaos. The previous Overlord of Lyrudrada was assassinated in her home in Stalker's Reach by the Reborn, and this act ignited anarchy and bloodshed across the city. Agents of the Reborn murder their enemies openly and promise power and authority to their allies. The leaders of the Reborn—primarily the owb prophet Veilisendri and his devoted follower, the caligni oracle Nephenie, who has declared herself to be the city's high priestess—have overthrown the longstanding checks and balances within the city. Now, nearly all the city's castes are forced to pay at least a token fealty to the Reborn while scrambling to grasp at authority over rival castes. The result is a roiling stew of skullduggery and scheming that frequently explodes into displays of shocking violence.

Government

Though there are dozens (and perhaps hundreds) of caste-clans within Lyrudrada, only a few principal groups remain after the Reborn's purge.

Amethyst Association: The mercantile caste-clan of Lyrudrada has retained much of its wealth and, although never particularly influential, much of its former sway within the city. This group operates primarily in Traders' Rift but has warehouses and emporiums throughout the city. The Amethyst Association is one of the few castes that allows limited membership to non-caligni, including a few duergar merchants from distant Hagegraf.

Bleakshore Council: This new organization is a secret society formed by the caligni of the Bleakshore district to oppose the rise of the Reborn. The council's activities were recently discovered by the Reborn and most of their members were killed or captured in a series of bloody raids. Only a single leader of the Bleakshore Council—the wealthy and influential caligni bard Aiyana—remains at large to oppose the Reborn.

Bloodshadows: Primarily composed of dark slayer killers and dark dancer spies, the Bloodshadows have always served as an assassins' guild of sorts for the city. This caste has allied with the Reborn and now primarily takes assignments to eliminate the Reborn's rivals or perceived threats. Bloodmaster Peyash Met-Amoo leads the caste from his fortress in Shadowheart, where he directs its members to eliminate former enemies and other up-and-coming caste leaders who threaten the Bloodshadows' role as the murderous right hand of the Reborn.

Rabble: The Rabble consists of scores of different caste-clans of Ragtown dark creepers, none of them influential or wealthy enough to warrant individual recognition within the city at large. Collectively, however, the Rabble is the largest caste-clan in the city by far. Unfortunately, members' uniform status belies their lack of solidarity: membership groups within the Rabble violently struggle among themselves for control of the larger group.

Reborn: The current center of power within Lyrudrada, this former secret society now openly operates from the formerly taboo site of Ancestors' Isle. Its leader, an owb prophet named Veilisendri, works to amass enough might

INTRODUCTION

CHAPTER 1:
REMNANTS OF THE DARK

CHAPTER 2:
GAME OF SHADOWS

CHAPTER 3:
FATE OF THE FORSAKEN

APPENDIX 1:
LYRUDRADA

APPENDIX 2:
BESTIARY

Lyrudrada

LYRUDRADA

CN small city

Corruption +7; **Crime** +7; **Economy** –5; **Law** –4; **Lore** +2; **Society** –5

Qualities filthy, insular, racially intolerant (surface dwellers), rule of might

Danger +25; **Disadvantages** anarchy

DEMOGRAPHICS

Government anarchy

Population 7,930 (5,811 dark creepers, 690 dark stalkers, 585 dark champions (see page 60), 405 dark dancers, 286 caligni, 68 dark slayers, 43 dark callers, 42 other)

NOTABLE NPCS

Bloodmaster Peyash Met-Amoo (CE male dark slayer[B2] rogue 8/assassin 5/shadowdancer 3)

High Priestess Nephenie (NE female caligni[B5] oracle[APG] 12)

Nomianna (CN female lampad[B4])

Patron Protector Ulloo Bao (LE male advanced elite dark stalker)

Slavemaster Turling Spindlestone (LE male duergar rogue 9/shadowdancer 4)

Veilisendri (NE owb prophet; see page 55)

MARKETPLACE

Base Value 3,000 gp; **Purchase Limit** 18,750 gp; **Spellcasting** 5th

Minor Items *+1 shadow chain shirt, +2 buckler*, elven chain, *+1 frost shortbow, +2 cold iron longsword*, clear spindle ioun stone, harp of charming, wand of acid arrow (50 charges), wand of cure moderate wounds (50 charges), wind fan; **Medium Items** +2 flaming dagger, deep red sphere ioun stone, manual of gainful exercise +1, ring of improved jumping, staff of healing, staff of fire, wand of bestow curse (50 charges); **Major Items** greater silent metamagic rod, pale green prism ioun stone

SETTLEMENT QUALITIES

Filthy Lyrudrada's citizens have little interest in sanitation or cleanliness, and the city streets reflect this fact. The filth discourages many merchants, travelers, and other visitors. (*Corruption +2, Crime +2, Economy –2, Law –2; decrease base value and purchase limit by 25%, lower spellcasting by 1 level*)

Rule of Might The dark folk of Lyrudrada serve their superiors not out of respect for tradition or laws, but purely out of fear and self-preservation. The citizens respect shows of force, but aren't open-minded or eager to make friends. (*Law +2, Society –2*)

to ascend to the ranks of the Forsaken, the lost gods of the Shadow Plane (see page 62).

Scuppers: The Scuppers form the largest dark creeper caste-clan of the Mudshore district. Their numbers include a handful of dark stalkers as leaders, but the caste retains its influence solely due to its size and its members' abilities as crafters and farmers. Second only to the Rabble in size, the Scuppers number well over 2,000 members, but they are just as disorganized as the Rabble.

Sentinels of the Shroud: One of the smallest caste-clans, the Sentinels operate out of their citadel of Highstone and serve as the primary military force and de facto protectors of Lyrudrada. Once the second most powerful caste in the city after the Stalker Society, the Sentinels currently retain much of their prestige despite being open targets of the Reborn. This is primarily due to the Sentinels' retreat to their defensible island, but also due to the charismatic nature of the Sentinels' leader, the Patron Protector Ulloo Bao. The majority of the Sentinels of the Shroud are dark champions (see page 60), although small coteries of dark callers, dark creepers, and dark dancers augment their forces.

Ulloo Bao

Stalker Society: An alliance of a dozen or so individual dark stalker caste-clans that occupy the district of Stalkers' Reach, the Stalker Society once represented the principal leadership of the city below the Sentinels of the Shroud. Intimidation and assassinations by the Reborn have put the Stalker Society back on its heels and scrambling for whatever power it can retain. All member clans of the Stalker Society have now ostensibly sworn fealty to the Reborn, but this group—and, by extension, all of Stalkers' Reach—is a cauldron of unrest and backstabbing. Assassinations occur daily, as each dark stalker clan leader attempts to rise above the others to control the Stalker Society and, perhaps, the now-vacant role of Overlord of Lyrudrada.

Toilers: The primary skilled labor caste-clan of the city, the Toilers occupy the Diggers' Delve district and oversee the hollowing of new cavern homes and access tunnels. A fairly insular caste, the Toilers nevertheless allow limited membership rights to non-caligni. In particular, a few dozen svirfneblin and pechs have been welcomed into the caste to assist in their construction projects and the handling of the many diggers (burrowing Darklands creatures) that the Toilers use in their projects.

Districts

Lyrudrada has long consisted of eight districts huddled on the shores and caverns surrounding the Grayfoam River. With the rise of the Reborn, a ninth district has been added to the city: the previously taboo Ancestors' Isle.

Ancestors' Isle: Lying at the center of the lake formed by the Grayfoam River, Ancestors' Isle has been taboo to the residents of Lyrudrada since Haramil's invasion millennia ago, when the fortress-shrine built into the column rising up from the island, the Forsaken Fane, was abandoned. The Reborn have occupied the Forsaken Fane, allying themselves with the ageless and powerful creatures therein, and have granted the cult's true believers the right to settle on the shores of the island. Ancestors' Isle is still the most sparsely settled of the city's districts, but new shanties for dark folk rise daily on the island's lower slopes.

Bleakshore: Although it is Lyrudrada's smallest district, Bleakshore has a reputation as the most welcoming to outsiders and, as a result, houses the largest concentration of caligni in the city. Here, they and their neighbors—predominantly dark stalkers—dwelled in relative peace. With the rise of the Reborn, several influential members of this district banded together in secret as the Bleakshore Council to oppose the Reborn, but the cult learned of the council's existence and moved swiftly to eliminate it. A number of the district's homes are now in ruins or are occupied by hostile forces that keep the rest of Bleakshore cowed through their presence.

Diggers' Delve: This remote shore of the city's central lake holds the dwellings of the Toilers caste-clan. Delver-Tor-Akato, a mountain-like fortress of fused stalagmites topped with towering turrets, serves as the region's most visible landmark and the home of **Amlgus Krith** (N male dark stalker expert 10), leader of the Toilers. Although predominantly inhabited by dark creepers, this neighborhood also houses a handful of svirfneblin and pechs. Several fenced side caverns hold tunnel worms, thoqquas, and other digging beasts trained by the Toilers.

Highstone: The smallest of Lyrudrada's districts, Highstone is a single island in the city's central lake, even smaller than Ancestor's Isle. The island is a single, massive stalagmite that was shorn off in some past calamity, creating a jagged surface several feet above the waterline. Safely out of reach of even the most powerful floods from the Grayfoam River, the residents of Highstone have built curtain walls and lesser fortifications all around their island. Only a single, well-defended pier juts from the island, and all visitors to Highstone are carefully monitored. Most of the city's dark champions inhabit this island, as it is the site of their grim training grounds and war academies, but the district's most influential figure is a dark stalker, Patron Protector Ulloo Bao. Ulloo had formerly coordinated the defense of Lyrudrada, stationing sentinels at each gate and coordinating patrols of the city. With the rise of the Reborn, Ulloo Bao and the Sentinels of the Shroud have largely retreated to their defensible district and welcome no intruders.

Mudshore: The downstream shore of the central lake endures most of the seasonal flooding, which deposits mineral-rich silt with each surge. The Scuppers caste tends large farms of subterranean fungus here, raising some varieties as food and others as building materials. Crafters of all types live here, including alchemists, coopers, potters, shipwrights, and tailors.

Ragtown: This massive district extends from the hovels and caves next to Shadowheart all the way to the farthest abodes where the Grayfoam exits the city. More than 4,000 dark creepers cram into this filthy maze of shanties, though many work as fishermen or as laborers throughout the rest of the city. The myriad factions of the Rabble hold sway here under the control of a handful of dark stalker demagogues. Small outbreaks of violence are common among rival groups; visitors are largely left alone, except by the district's many skilled pickpockets.

Shadowheart: This dark district is the home of the Bloodshadows caste, ruled by Bloodmaster Peyash Met-Amoo from the Tower of Ksham near the district's southern gate. The district is easily identified by the dull red paint used to decorate buildings and cavern walls, making entire urban vistas seem drenched in blood. Other than the Bloodshadows, the most numerous inhabitants of this district are dark creepers of the Rabble caste, who spend their days currying favor, performing menial tasks, or attempting to redirect the Bloodshadows' murderous attentions elsewhere.

Stalkers' Reach: The most isolated of Lyrudrada's districts, Stalkers' Reach is populated primarily by dark stalkers and the dark creepers that each household keeps as servants or errand-runners. The dark stalkers of this district have long maintained a sense of smug superiority in their leadership of the city, but find their recent overthrow by the Reborn both humbling and terrifying. Stalkers' Reach is now one of the city's most dangerous districts, as kidnappings, murders, and sabotage are commonplace. The Overlord's Manor remains abandoned at the north end of this district: the Reborn don't need it to demonstrate their authority, and no one else dares to occupy it for fear of consolidating their enemies against them.

Traders' Rift: Lyrudrada's most cosmopolitan district and the headquarters of the Amethyst Association, Traders' Rift consists primarily of merchant residences, warehouses, and shops. Merchants from across the Darklands—and, occasionally, from the surface world—engage in spirited trading here, out of sight of the rest of the city. Although Trader's Rift is split in half by the Grayfoam River, a coalition of spellcasters long ago created an ingenious crystal-roofed tunnel underneath the river to connect the two sides. The view of the river churning just overhead can be unsettling, but the tunnel is safer to use than the makeshift ferries and rafts above.

Notable Sites

The following locations either are significant to the residents of Lyrudrada or are sites the PCs are likely to visit in the *Cradle of Night* adventure.

1. City Gates. Although not every tunnel providing access to Lyrudrada bears a gate, the city's 10 gates are indicated on the poster map. Each of these gates is constructed of sturdy stone hewn from the surrounding rock by skilled members of the Toilers caste. Twenty-foot-tall towers topped with crenellations flank a 15-foot-wide gate made of thick planks of hardened fungus bound with heavy iron fittings.

2. Aiyana's Estate. An opulent manor in the Bleakshore district, the estate of the caligni bard Aiyana has been occupied by her family for many generations. This site is detailed beginning on page 21.

3. Seer's Cavern. The ceiling of this large, peaceful cavern is covered with glowworms that give it the appearance of twinkling stars. A gentle stream fills this cavern, draining into the Grayfoam through the Mudshore district. The denizens of Mudshore consider the cavern to be a holy place, and they occasionally seek the counsel of the fey seer on the island at the cavern's center. This site is detailed beginning on page 29.

4. Brokerage. The cloaker Shevarimarr is one of Lyrudrada's most notorious information brokers. His shop, nestled against a cavern wall in Trader's Rift, is detailed beginning on page 30.

5. Sadist Spires. Few wealthy estates stand amid the squalor of Ragtown, but even the most desperate burglar gives the paired stalagmites known as the Sadist Spires a wide berth. The drider Ezurkian lurks in these spires, performing vile experiments on captives and on prisoners "gifted" to him by influential caligni who want to dispose of rivals in as gruesome a method as possible. This site is detailed beginning on page 33.

6. Forsaken Fane. The temple-fortress at the center of Ancestors' Isle is the headquarters of the Reborn and the lair of the owb prophet at its dark heart. This site is detailed beginning on page 41.

7. Grayfoam River. This wide, slow-moving river connects several distant subterranean communities, although it is prone to surges that flood low-lying areas and capsize river travelers; the foaming torrents these surges produce give the river its name. Its water is thick with bitter, gray silt. The river is rarely more than 20 feet in depth, except in the large basin in the center of Lyrudrada. There, the Grayfoam reaches depths of up to 80 feet, and its cold depths conceal ruins and monsters unknown even to the caligni fisherfolk who ply its waters.

BESTIARY

Dark Champion

This gaunt humanoid's body is entirely cased in black plate armor. Its open-faced helm reveals its pale skin and shallow, fleshy hollows where its eyes should be.

DARK CHAMPION   CR 5

XP 1,600

LE Medium humanoid (dark folk)

Init +1; **Senses** blindsight 90 ft.; Perception +8

DEFENSE

AC 20, touch 11, flat-footed 19 (+9 armor, +1 Dex)

hp 59 (7d8+28)

Fort +9, **Ref** +3, **Will** +4

Immune gaze attacks, sight-based attacks, visual effects

Weaknesses vulnerable to sonic

OFFENSE

Speed 30 ft.

Melee mwk greatsword +11/+6 (2d6+4/19–20)

Ranged heavy crossbow +8 (1d10/19–20)

Special Attacks death throes

STATISTICS

Str 17, **Dex** 12, **Con** 18, **Int** 8, **Wis** 11, **Cha** 9

Base Atk +7; **CMB** +10; **CMD** 21

Feats Cleave, Disruptive, Iron Will, Power Attack

Skills Perception +8, Stealth +2; **Racial Modifiers** +4 Perception, +4 Stealth

Languages Undercommon, Dark Folk

SQ champion armor, fighter training

ECOLOGY

Environment any underground

Organization solitary, patrol (2–6), or platoon (8–16)

Treasure NPC gear (full plate, masterwork greatsword, heavy crossbow with 20 bolts, other treasure)

SPECIAL ABILITIES

Champion Armor (Ex) A dark champion's speed is not reduced for wearing armor.

Death Throes (Su) A slain dark champion combusts in an explosive flash that destroys its armor but not its other gear. All creatures within a 10-foot radius burst take 3d6 points of fire damage and an additional 2d6 points of piercing damage (Reflex DC 17 half). The save DC is Constitution-based.

Fighter Training (Ex) Dark champions are proficient with all simple and martial weapons and with all armor and shields. They have a base attack bonus equal to their Hit Dice and can select combat feats that have fighter levels as a prerequisite, treating their Hit Dice as their fighter level for that purpose.

The rare dark folk children born without eyes are assigned to the dark champion caste and begin a life of rigor, privation, and martial training. Their armor is typically bolted to their bodies in sections and removed only rarely. Most other dark folk appreciate the discipline and might of dark champions, but they treat them with wary respect.

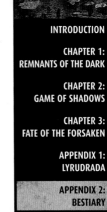

INTRODUCTION

CHAPTER 1:
REMNANTS OF THE DARK

CHAPTER 2:
GAME OF SHADOWS

CHAPTER 3:
FATE OF THE FORSAKEN

APPENDIX 1:
LYRUDRADA

APPENDIX 2:
BESTIARY

Nimbral Child

This emaciated humanoid is barely visible in a swirl of engulfing shadow. Its eyes and mouth reveal a burning void within its head.

NIMBRAL CHILD	CR 11

XP 12,800

CE Medium outsider (evil, extraplanar)

Init +8; **Senses** darkvision 60 ft., see in darkness; Perception +19

DEFENSE

AC 26, touch 20, flat-footed 21 (+5 deflection, +4 Dex, +1 dodge, +6 natural)

hp 133 (14d10+56)

Fort +8, **Ref** +15, **Will** +13

Defensive Abilities dark nimbus; **Immune** blindness, cold, poison; **Resist** acid 10, electricity 10, fire 10

Weaknesses light sensitivity

OFFENSE

Speed 40 ft., climb 40 ft.

Melee 2 claws +18 (2d8+3 plus 4d6 cold)

Special Attacks breath of the void (30-ft. cone, 10d6 cold damage plus slowed, Reflex DC 21 for half, usable every 1d4 rounds), penumbral web (+18 ranged, DC 21, 14 hp)

Spell-Like Abilities (CL 14th; concentration +19)

At will—*deeper darkness, greater teleport* (self plus 50 lbs. of objects only)

3/day—*shadow conjuration* (DC 19), *shadow evocation* (DC 20), *shadow walk* (DC 21), *spell turning*

1/day—*greater shadow evocation* (DC 23), *power word blind*

STATISTICS

Str 16, **Dex** 19, **Con** 18, **Int** 13, **Wis** 14, **Cha** 21

Base Atk +14; **CMB** +17; **CMD** 37

Feats Dodge, Improved Initiative, Iron Will, Lightning Reflexes, Mobility, Spring Attack, Weapon Finesse

Skills Bluff +22, Climb +11, Intimidate +22, Knowledge (planes) +18, Perception +19, Spellcraft +18, Stealth +21, Use Magic Device +22

Languages telepathy 120 ft.

ECOLOGY

Environment any land (Shadow Plane)

Organization solitary or gloaming (2–6)

Treasure none

SPECIAL ABILITIES

Breath of the Void (Su) A nimbral child's breath weapon is a blast of howling, frigid winds drawn from the void. A nimbral child cannot use this ability while it is within an area of bright light. A creature that fails its saving throw against the nimbral child's breath weapon is slowed (as per the *slow* spell) for 1d4 rounds. The save DC is Constitution-based.

Dark Nimbus (Su) Shadows swirl around a nimbral child, granting it concealment from attacks and a deflection bonus to its Armor Class equal to its Charisma modifier.

Penumbral Web (Su) Eight times per day as a standard action, a nimbral child can project gray, shadowy webs as per the web universal monster rule (*Pathfinder RPG Bestiary* 305). In addition to being subject to the webs' entangling effect, any creature not native to the Shadow Plane touching a penumbral web takes 1d6 points of Strength damage and is paralyzed for 1d4 rounds (Fortitude DC 21 to halve the damage and negate the paralysis). A nimbral child can also create sheets of penumbral webbing. These sheets do not burn but can be pushed aside, although touching them affects a target as per a successful penumbral web attack. If a nimbral child is destroyed, all penumbral webs it has created dissolve in 1d4 rounds. The save DC is Constitution-based.

Powerful practitioners of shadow magic sometimes summon these kin of the enigmatic shining children (*Pathfinder RPG Bestiary 2* 245) for their own nefarious purposes, but never without risk.

Owb Prophet

This creature resembles the skeletal torso of a winged, four-armed giant draped in tatters of liquid shadow.

OWB PROPHET   **CR 13**

XP 25,600

NE Large outsider (extraplanar)

Init +10; **Senses** darkvision 60 ft., see in darkness; Perception +23

DEFENSE

AC 28, touch 16, flat-footed 21 (+6 Dex, +1 dodge, +12 natural, −1 size)

hp 184 (16d10+96); fast healing 5

Fort +16, **Ref** +16, **Will** +11

DR 10/magic; **Immune** bleed, cold, disease, mind-affecting effects, poison

Weaknesses light sensitivity

OFFENSE

Speed 5 ft., fly 60 ft. (perfect)

Melee 4 claws +21 (2d6+6/19–20 plus 1d6 cold)

Ranged burning cold +21 touch (3d6 cold plus entangle)

Special Attacks curse of darkness

Space 10 ft.; **Reach** 10 ft.

Spell-Like Abilities (CL 16th; concentration +21)

Constant—*blur*

At will—*deeper darkness, detect thoughts* (DC 17), *dust of twilight*[APG] (DC 17), *ray of enfeeblement* (DC 16), *shadow step*[UM], *silence* (DC 17)

3/day—*dominate person* (DC 20), *plane shift* (to or from the Shadow Plane only; DC 20), quickened *shadow step*[UM], *shadow evocation* (DC 20)

1/day—*greater shadow conjuration* (DC 22), *shadow walk* (DC 20)

STATISTICS

Str 22, **Dex** 23, **Con** 22, **Int** 17, **Wis** 18, **Cha** 21

Base Atk +16; **CMB** +23; **CMD** 40

Feats Combat Reflexes, Dodge, Flyby Attack, Improved Initiative, Iron Will, Point-Blank Shot, Quicken Spell-Like Ability (*shadow step*), Vital Strike

Skills Bluff +24, Diplomacy +16, Fly +23, Intimidate +24, Knowledge (planes, religion) +22, Perception +23, Sense Motive +23, Spellcraft +22, Stealth +21

Languages Aklo, Common, Dark Folk, Undercommon (can't speak); telepathy 100 ft.

SQ deific, Forsaken patron (Husk)

ECOLOGY

Environment any land or underground (Shadow Plane)

Organization solitary

Treasure standard

SPECIAL ABILITIES

Burning Cold (Su) An owb prophet can conjure a ball of flickering flames and hurl it at an opponent as an attack action, or hurl four balls of flame as a full-attack action. These flames are ranged touch attacks with a range of 120 feet with no range increment. Each flame deals 3d6 points of cold damage. Any creature struck by the flames must succeed at a DC 24 Reflex save or become entangled for 1d6 rounds. The save DC is Constitution-based.

Curse of Darkness (Su) With a touch, an owb prophet can make bright light unbearable to the victim. A creature touched must succeed at a DC 23 Fortitude save or gain the light blindness weakness. This ability also robs the victim of its coloration, leaving the creature and its equipment washed-out shades of gray. This effect can be removed with *break enchantment* or *remove curse*, unless the target has the dark folk subtype, in which case the effect can be removed only by *wish* or similar magic. The save DC is Charisma-based.

Deific An owb prophet can grant divine spells to its worshippers. Granting spells doesn't require any specific action on the owb prophet's behalf. Owb prophets grant access to the domains of Darkness, Evil, Madness, and Trickery. Their symbols and favored weapons vary based on the owb prophet's Forsaken patron.

Forsaken Patron Each owb prophet serves as a conduit to one of the distant, shadowy demigods known as the Forsaken. Forsaken patrons are described below, and each patron grants the owb prophet additional abilities. The choice of Forsaken patron cannot be changed.

Few remember that the Shadow Plane once had its own demigods, akin to the Eldest of the First World. Called the Forsaken, these mysterious, evil entities had a direct hand in shaping the caligni race but then vanished for unknown reasons. Although caligni cannot call upon the Forsaken, the sinister owbs (*Pathfinder RPG Bestiary 4* 210) can still reach these distant demigods by performing esoteric rituals in remote temples on the Shadow Plane.

An owb who successfully contacts one of the Forsaken gains a fragment of the demigod's power and forms a permanent connection to that Forsaken patron. This contact causes dramatic physical changes, often forcing the owb to swell in size and sprout additional limbs, but the most significant change is that the owb becomes a divine conduit. Known as owb prophets, these god-touched beings grant spells to faithful worshippers on behalf of their Forsaken patrons. Unfortunately for the Forsaken, owb prophets don't pass along this divine energy gladly, always seeking a way to hoard it for themselves. The most cunning owb prophets develop long-term plans to ascend to the status of demigod independently and join the ranks of the Forsaken. No owb prophet has yet acquired sufficient spiritual energy to make this leap, but the first to succeed would be more than a peer to the distant Forsaken—it would be the only active Forsaken in the multiverse.

Forsaken Patrons

Although the Forsaken do not have worshippers as most demigods do, owb prophets commit themselves to these mysterious entities and gain the indicated benefits.

The most noteworthy Forsaken are described below as they once appeared; their current forms and powers remain purely speculation.

Enkaar, the Malformed Prisoner (NE Forsaken of fetters, lethargy, and physical corruption): Left to die in a festering prison on the Shadow Plane, Enkaar eventually emerged as a mutated horror draped in rusted chains. Enkaar's owb prophets are immune to petrification and paralysis, gain two wing attacks as natural attacks, and can use *excruciating deformation*[UM] at will as a spell-like ability. Enkaar's symbol is a pus-encrusted fetter, and its favored weapon is the spiked chain.

Eyes That Watch (NE Forsaken of feelings of inferiority, felines, and strangers): None can fully describe the Forsaken known as Eyes That Watch, as it appeared only as a trio of feline eyes staring from shadows with an arrogant gaze. Eyes That Watch's owb prophets gain blindsight with a range of 60 feet, can always act in the surprise round, and can use *burning gaze*[APG] at will as a spell-like ability. The flames from this spell-like ability are always a dull yellow and never shed more than dim light. Eyes That Watch's symbol is three feline eyes, and its favored weapon is the dagger.

Grasping Iovett (CE Forsaken of accidents, parasites, and reckless lust): Clad only in heavy black silks that shifted to reveal sensual forms of an indescribable variety, Grasping Iovett's touch left painful welts and tick infestations. Iovett's owb prophets are immune to disease and poison, cannot be grappled unless they choose to be, and automatically succeed at combat maneuver checks and Escape Artist checks to escape a grapple or pin. They can use *eruptive pustules*[UM] at will as a spell-like ability. Iovett's symbol is a stylized tick on a swatch of silk, and its favored weapon is the short sword.

Husk (NE Forsaken of emptiness, loneliness, and narcissism): Husk was an attractive, androgynous humanoid whose joints were gaps that revealed the Forsaken to be entirely hollow beneath paper-thin skin. Husk's owb prophets are immune to bleed, disease, mind-affecting effects, and poison, and they can use *silence* at will as a spell-like ability. Husk's symbol is an empty humanoid outline with hands outstretched, and its favored weapon is the short sword.

Lady Razor (NE Forsaken of family strife, suspicion, and vengeance): A stern magistrate among the Forsaken, Lady Razor forbade showing kindness or mercy to family members. Lady Razor's owb prophets are proficient with all slashing weapons, never take penalties on attack rolls when fighting with multiple slashing weapons, and can use *keen edge* at will as a spell-like ability. Lady Razor's symbol is a gavel crossed with a bloody razor, and her favored weapon is the dagger.

Reshmit of the Heavy Voice (CE Forsaken of broken things, forgetting, and unexpected violence): Reshmit was a Gargantuan shadowy form whose softest touch landed like a hammer blow and whose rumbling voice could shred steel. Reshmit's owb prophets emanate an aura of forgetfulness within 30 feet; each creature in the aura other than owb prophets must attempt a Will save (DC = 10 + half the owb prophet's Hit Dice + the owb prophet's Charisma modifier) each round or lose one prepared spell or available spell slot. They can use *shatter* at will as a spell-like ability. Reshmit's symbol is a torn steel plate, and his favored weapon is the morningstar.

Thalaphyrr Martyr-Minder (LE Forsaken of failed heroics, imprisonment, and squandered time): Thalaphyrr guarded the prisons where the Forsaken kept their would-be usurpers and destroyers. Creatures within 30 feet of Thalaphyrr's owb prophets cannot benefit from morale bonuses. In addition, his owb prophets can use *slow* at will as a spell-like ability. Thalaphyrr's symbol is a pair of hands grasping a set of prison bars, and his favored weapon is the spear.

INTRODUCTION

CHAPTER 1:
REMNANTS OF THE DARK

CHAPTER 2:
GAME OF SHADOWS

CHAPTER 3:
OF THE FORSAKEN

APPENDIX 1:
LYRUDRADA

APPENDIX 2:
BESTIARY